I0519724

Maritime Energy Management in UAE by the Use of Green Practices at UAE Companies and Ports

By:

Mustafa Nejem

Abstract

This research is focused on sustainable practices within the UAE maritime industry that examine the embracement and collective impact of environment-friendly initiatives on marine efficiency. The purpose of this research is to determine the extent to which sustainable energy is implemented at UAE ports and how these initiatives are a source of enhancing efficiency. The research analyses sustainable practices of solar power, wind energy, innovative propulsion systems, and vessel design implemented to a smaller extent by the UAE shipping companies and ports. To explore more on the application, an extensive literature review of research is conducted. The review has identified the gaps in implementing various practices in the long term that can induce sustainability in maritime energy management at UAE ports. The research has employed quantitative research design in the form of surveys and statistical analyses that explore the short-term embracement levels by ports and shipping companies. The research findings have revealed substantial adoption except for already established vessel designs. Furthermore, the findings recommend integrating strategies, policy advocacy, research investment, training, stakeholder engagement, and continuous improvement within the maritime energy sector. Hence, the study positions the UAE as a global leader in sustainable maritime operations that underscore the transformative potential of industry-wide commitment to environmental responsibility.

Keywords: maritime, energy management, UAE, UAE ports, green practices, UAE companies, efficiency, solar power, wind energy, propulsion system, hull design and maintenance.

Table of Contents

List of Tables

List of Figures

Chapter 1

INTRODUCTION TO THE STUDY

The ports of the UAE are affected greatly due to changes in the environment and the decline in sea levels. The increase in climate change concern has caused green initiatives to be implemented, but it is not enough to cater to the challenges. Instead, there is a need for green practices to be endorsed at the seaports. This initiative aids in maintaining the health of the sea by taking actions at seaports that can manage the influence of pollution i.e., optimise the air quality index by reducing particulate matter. UAE ports are located at the center of the trade and transportation of the world's maritime infrastructure which drives them towards economic stability at the cost of affecting the environment due to incessant trade. The research is conducted to investigate the establishment of environmentally friendly practices at UAE companies and ports to improve efficiency. These practices include solar power, wind energy, propulsion systems, hull design, and maintenance. However, like many other ports worldwide, the traditional operations of UAE ships and maritime management heavily rely on fossil fuels that contribute to greenhouse gas emissions and air pollution. For global environmental concerns and international regulations, UAE ports have initiated the adoption of sustainable practices aimed at reducing their carbon footprint and enhancing energy efficiency. The UAE boasts an expansive coastline and vibrant ports, acknowledging the imperative to adopt robust green initiatives. While there is a recognition of the significance of these endeavors in safeguarding the marine environment, fostering sustainable development, and adhering to international environmental standards, the current implementation remains somewhat constrained. Despite the existing efforts, there is room for an enhanced and more comprehensive restructuring of these green initiatives to amplify their impact and ensure a more substantial commitment to environmental sustainability. To address these challenges, the UAE needs to take significant steps to transition its ports towards more sustainable and environmentally friendly practices, which include key initiatives at the government level. The first key initiative the government should take is the use of solar power as an energy source to become increasingly prevalent at UAE ports. In this regard, solar panels should be installed on port facilities and vessels to harness the abundant sunlight in the region, thereby reducing reliance on non-renewable energy sources and mitigating greenhouse gas emissions as a few private vendors have done in UAE (Kandiyil, 2022). Secondly, wind turbines and wind farms have been integrated into port infrastructure by private entities for harnessing the powerful winds in coastal areas where this renewable energy source not only reduces the carbon footprint but also contributes to a diversified and cleaner energy mix (Arun Kumar et al., 2020). However, they are done by private companies and the government support is negligible for wind farm initiatives. Thirdly, innovations in propulsion systems are important to enhance energy efficiency and reduce the environmental impact of maritime transportation, which the government and policymakers should involve in their practice. The use of cleaner propulsion technologies including LNG (liquefied natural gas) and electric propulsion to gain momentum in the UAE ports ultimately reduces emissions and improves efficiency (Ash & Scarbrough, 2019). Lastly, optimising vessel design, encompassing hull considerations, and ensuring meticulous maintenance practices can significantly enhance fuel efficiency and reduce drag, thereby minimising the environmental footprint of maritime activities (Dewan & Godina, 2023). However, it is important to note that these initiatives, while commendable, currently operate on a smaller scale and are insufficient to counterbalance the environmental impact of maritime activities in which the UAE is actively involved. So, through the adoption of these green initiatives, UAE companies and ports aim to not only improve their environmental performance but also adhere to international regulations and address global environmental concerns. Hence, the research seeks to assess the small-scale implementation of environmentally friendly practices that have been adopted by UAE companies and ports to know about the efficiency of green initiatives. The following is an explication of the background, problem statement, purpose, research question, and theoretical foundations of the research. The research expounds on key ideas, definitions, assumptions, scope, delimitations, and limitations of the study, setting the groundwork to conduct research that explores the positive impact of green practices on maritime energy management at UAE ports.

1.1. Prologue

UAE has 12 commercial ports with 80 million tons of cargo. The ports have been working for more than 40 years and have contributed to the reduction in sea levels. According to a report, UAE ports are vulnerable to shallow sloping seaports by 35 cm per km, which means that they are greatly affected by the poor environment such that there is a need for green initiatives to cater to climate change and ensure maritime energy management (Subraelu et al., 2022). UAE as a nation with a rich history of trade and maritime transportation needs to embrace environmentally responsible practices within its ports to become more pronounced (Viswanathan, 2022). UAE port facilities even today rely heavily on fossil fuels that contribute to greenhouse gas emissions and air pollution affecting the air quality index. In response to growing environmental concerns and international regulations, the UAE has embarked on a journey at a smaller scale to transition its ports towards sustainability that aims to reduce the impact of pollution. UAE has set the reduction target to 23.5% by 2030; this is to help the world counter climate change by taking appropriate actions. It is because UAE is a key player in the maritime industry and participated in global warming due to industrialization (UNEP, 2019). This research seeks to shed light on the extent to which environmentally friendly practices have been adopted by UAE companies and ports. It also explains how these initiatives have impacted both efficiency and the overall health of the marine environment. There are four key pillars to this transformation that are adopted, these pillars include solar power, wind energy, innovative propulsion systems, and optimised vessel design and maintenance. The implications of these green initiatives extend beyond mere environmental responsibility where they also align with international regulations and address global environmental concerns. Hence, through these practices, UAE companies and ports aim not only to improve their environmental performance but also to ensure the short-term sustainability of their operations along with creating a greener, more sustainable future for both the nation and the wider global community. This research, in this context, aims to see the short-term extent to which these green initiatives are endorsed at UAE ports.

1.2. Background of the Study

The maritime energy management sector faces significant challenges specifically in the context of environmental sustainability and climate change. The consequences of climate change pose a direct threat to the operation and health of seaports worldwide. These threats include rising sea levels, extreme weather events, and ecological disruptions that need a proper solution (Siegel, 2019). The UAE partakes in the trade that affects world pollution, which is a symbol of the broader environmental challenges that are faced by maritime hubs across the globe. The following findings are about the evolving landscape of maritime operations and the imperative to adopt environmentally friendly practices within the UAE ports.

1.2.1. Maritime Industry and Environmental Impact

The maritime industry has been a driving force behind global trade and economic growth that accounts for approximately 80% of the world's trade by volume and over 70% by value (Koilo, 2019). However, this significant contribution comes at a cost to the environment i.e., fossil fuels resulting in greenhouse emissions. The International Maritime Organisation (IMO) estimated that shipping is responsible for approximately 2.2% of global greenhouse gas emissions (IMO, 2019). Moreover, emissions from shipping vessels have been associated with various adverse environmental effects that include ocean acidification, habitat destruction, and oil spills (Walker et al., 2019, p. 27). The continued growth of global trade has influenced these environmental challenges that makes it important to find sustainable solutions.

1.2.2. Global Concern of Climate Change

Climate change is a global issue that is intrinsically associated with the health of the world's oceans and their impact on seaports. Sea-level rise is a result of various interrelated factors, including but not limited to the melting of polar ice caps and the thermal expansion of seawater. This phenomenon poses a direct threat to low-lying coastal areas along with many port cities leading to inundation, erosion, and the salinization of freshwater resources (Kekeh et al., 2020). The influences of rising sea levels are not limited to coastal communities but also extend to port infrastructure along with their ability to operate efficiently. Therefore, the risk of damage and disruption to ports, including the potential loss of critical infrastructure, is a pressing concern. This underscores the imperative need for the integration of sustainable practices to mitigate such risks and enhance the resilience of maritime operations.

1.2.3. United Arab Emirates and Maritime Significance

UAE is a nation that has greatly benefited from its strategic geographic location at the crossroads of international trade routes which makes it a vital hub for global commerce. The UAE's ports like Jebel Ali and Khalifa port have played a pivotal role in connecting the East and West facilitating the movement of goods and passengers (Akhavan, 2019). The UAE is a nation that is characterized by rapid economic growth and development, especially in the fields of energy, construction, and infrastructure which are heavily reliant on maritime transportation (Livsey, 2019).

1.2.4. Initiatives for Sustainable Maritime Practices

It is important to recognize the significance of UAE's ports and the environmental challenges associated with maritime operations where they have embarked on a journey to transition their ports toward sustainability. The government and industry stakeholders have to undertake several key initiatives to reduce the environmental footprint of maritime activities and enhance energy efficiency. These initiatives encompass a range of sustainable practices that include the use of solar power as a renewable energy source along with the integration of wind turbines and wind farms into port infrastructure, innovations in propulsion systems, and optimisation of vessel design and maintenance.

Hence, these initiatives hold great promise as it is essential to assess the extent to which they have been adopted by UAE companies and ports and their actual impact on efficiency and the marine environment. Thus, this research aims to bridge the existing knowledge gap through a comprehensive exploration of the positive impact of these green practices on maritime energy management in UAE ports.

1.3. Problem Statement

The research addresses the pressing concern of the maritime industry in the UAE, which faces environmental challenges due to reliance on fossil fuels that contribute to greenhouse gas emissions, air pollution, and marine pollution. With a significant ecological footprint, the impact of industry on the region's coastline and marine ecosystems is substantial. The urgent need for sustainable practices is underscored by the escalating threats of climate change, rising sea levels, and extreme weather events. The research aims to evaluate the short-term extent of adoption and impact of green initiatives by different organisations where the practices are renewable energy integration, innovative propulsion systems, and optimised vessel design. These practices within the UAE's maritime sector are crucial to safeguard both economic interests and environmental sustainability.

1.4. Purpose of the Study

The purpose of this study is to use quantitative techniques to prove that green initiatives are applied at the ports of the UAE by private organisations at a short-term level. However, the government and regulatory authorities need to take initiatives as well due to the impact of UAE ports on the sustainability of the environment. The study aims to assess the extent to which changes are endorsed and determine the scope of new changes that exist to increase the efficiency of initiatives at the ports. The research also aims to verify the efficiency of green initiatives at UAE ports and their role in optimising the climate. The focus of the study is to prove the need for UAE ports to opt for solar energy, wind energy, innovative propulsion systems, and vessel design in entirety to reduce their carbon footprint while maintaining their economic activity as a trade hub.

1.5. Research Question(s) and Hypotheses

The research question based on the findings of the background and analysis of the topic is as follows:

RQ: How environment-friendly practices of solar power, wind energy, innovative propulsion systems, and optimised vessel design and maintenance are embraced in the short term by UAE ports and shipping companies, and what is the impact of these initiatives on the efficiency and health of the marine environment?

H00: There is no embracement of environment-friendly practices of solar power, wind energy, innovative propulsion systems, and optimised vessel design and maintenance in the short term by UAE ports and shipping companies, and no significant impact of these initiatives on the efficiency and health of the marine environment.

H01: There is a practical embracement of environment-friendly practices of solar power, wind energy, innovative propulsion systems, and optimised vessel design and maintenance in the short term by UAE ports and shipping companies, and a positive significant impact of these initiatives on the efficiency and health of the marine environment.

Based on these hypotheses, the inclination is expected to lean towards the alternate hypothesis, given the substantial efforts incorporated by UAE ports. These efforts align with global environmental concerns and adhere to international regulations. Moreover, the health of the marine environment in the UAE is expected to benefit from the adoption of green initiatives as these practices will result in reduced emissions, minimised pollution, and the preservation of fragile ecosystems that contribute to the ecological well-being of coastal regions and marine ecosystems. Furthermore, the findings of this research have implications for the broader Middle East and Gulf regions as they provide a valuable framework for sustainable maritime practices in the region. Lastly, the research question and hypothesis are imperative for evidence-based recommendations that allow policymakers and industry leaders to promote a maritime industry that is both economically resilient and ecologically responsible in the UAE and potentially beyond.

These hypotheses form the foundation for the research study and the subsequent data collection along with analysis that validate or refute them. The research makes use of a combination of quantitative framework to assess the extent of adoption of green initiatives along with their impact on efficiency, and their influence on the health of the marine environment in the UAE. The ultimate goal of the research is to contribute to the body of knowledge that surrounds sustainable practices in the maritime industry and provide practical insights for stakeholders and policymakers that strive to strike a balance between environmental responsibility and operational efficiency in the UAE and similar regions. Hence, this research question and hypothesis are properly structured to develop a proper quantitative framework by the use of surveys among maritime industry workers of UAE that helps to know about the situation at UAE ports.

1.6. Theoretical Foundation

The theoretical foundation for this research is based on three key frameworks that are innovation diffusion theory, sustainable development theory, and environment policy theory. Innovation diffusion theory can help to understand how and why environment-friendly practices like the adoption of renewable energy sources and innovative propulsion systems are adopted within the maritime industry in the UAE. The theory provides insights into the factors that impact the rate of adoption and diffusion of these green initiatives. Secondly, sustainable development theory can be valuable to assess the impact of environment-friendly practices on the health of the marine environment. It provides a framework to evaluate how these practices contribute to the sustainability of maritime operations along with the preservation of ecological balance in coastal regions. Lastly, environmental policy theory helps to analyse the role of government policies and regulations in shaping the adoption of green initiatives in the maritime sector. This theory can also explicate how international environmental standards and regulations impact the decision-making process of UAE companies and ports. The following is an explanation of each theory in the context of the research topic that helps to explore the conceptual and theoretical framework of the study.

1.6.1. Innovation Diffusion Theory

Innovation diffusion theory was developed by Everett Rogers in 1962 (Quinlan, 2008). This theory served as a comprehensive framework for understanding the adoption of innovations within a social system. In the context of the research question on environmentally friendly practices in the maritime industry of UAE, this theory imparts valuable insights into the factors that influence the uptake of innovations, specifically for the adoption of renewable energy sources and innovative propulsion systems. According to Rogers, the diffusion process of an innovation includes five key stages that are knowledge, persuasion, decision, implementation, and confirmation (Miller, 2015). In the first stage i.e., knowledge, the individuals within the maritime industry in the UAE become aware of the existence of environment-friendly practices. This happens due to exposure to successful research studies, industry conferences, and government initiatives that promote sustainable maritime solutions. The second stage of persuasion involves the communication of the benefits and advantages of these green initiatives. At this stage, stakeholders can be influenced by the potential economic savings, positive environmental impacts, and alignment with global sustainability goals. The third stage is the decision, which marks the point at which key decision-makers within the industry commit to adopting these environmentally friendly practices. This decision is influenced by various factors, which include the perceived compatibility of the innovation with existing practices along with its complexity, and the potential for trialability and observability. The fourth stage is implementation, which includes the actual adoption and integration of innovations into the maritime operations of UAE companies and ports. During this stage, the challenges include cost, technological compatibility, and regulatory compliance, which can influence the successful implementation of these practices. The final stage is confirmation, which assesses the extent to which the adopted innovations meet the expectations of the stakeholders. The positive outcomes in the context of expectations are increased energy efficiency, reduced emissions, and economic benefits that reinforce the adoption of these environmentally friendly practices. These outcomes provide a positive feedback loop for future innovations. Thus, the application of this theory to the maritime industry implicates the characteristics of the innovation itself, the communication channels used, the structure of the social system, and the external environment that plays a key role in shaping the adoption process.

1.6.2. Sustainable Development Theory

Sustainable development theory is rooted in the Brundtland Report's definition of sustainable development as "development that meets the needs of the present without compromising the ability of future generations to meet their own needs" (Alketbi, 2023). This theory offers a robust framework to evaluate the impact of environmentally friendly practices on the health of the marine environment concerning the UAE's maritime industry (Alketbi, 2023). This theory has recognized the interconnectedness of economic, social, and environmental factors that accentuate the importance of achieving a harmonious balance among them. In the UAE's maritime sector, the application of the theory includes a critical examination of the adoption of practices that include the use of optimisgreen initiatives and maintenance that help to ascertain their contribution to the long-term sustainability of maritime operations (Jan et al., 2022). These findings implicate that the maritime industry is a vital component of global trade that faces considerable challenges in reconciling economic growth with environmental conservation. UAE has an extensive coastline and reliance on maritime trade, which induces paramount importance for the preservation of marine ecosystems. This theory embodies the utilization of renewable energy sources, particularly solar power and wind energy. Aligned with the principles of sustainable development, it serves to mitigate the environmental impact associated with traditional fossil fuel-based operations. The integration of solar panels on port facilities and vessels in the UAE has exemplified a commitment to reduce reliance on non-renewable energy sources that address climate change concerns and contribute to a sustainable energy future. The installation of wind turbines and wind farms in coastal areas further accentuates the commitment to diversify the energy mix and reduce the carbon footprint which is aligned with the emphasis of the theory on environmental conservation (Skjærseth et al., 2023). Another application is the use of propulsion systems at UAE ports that represent a tangible effort toward the reduction of emissions and improvement in energy efficiency. This theory posits that economic activities should be conducted within the ecological limits of the environment. In this regard, the transition to cleaner propulsion technologies in the UAE's maritime sector reflects a commitment to minimise the environmental footprint of maritime activities that helps to ensure the long-term health of coastal regions. Lastly, there is a need to make use of optimised vessel design along with maintenance practices in the maritime industry. These practices are based on the theoretical vision to meet present needs without compromising the ability of future generations to meet their needs criteria. which emphasises the importance of responsible resource management and ecological stewardship. Henceforth, this theory has implemented a robust framework to evaluate the impact of environmentally friendly practices on the health of the marine environment in the UAE's maritime industry where the adoption of renewable energy sources, innovative propulsion systems, and optimised vessel design and maintenance practices reflects a commitment to achieve a harmonious balance between economic growth and environmental conservation.

1.6.3. Environment Policy Theory

Environmental policy theory is a framework that examines the development, implementation, and impact of government policies along with regulations on environmental issues (Leipold et al., 2019). This framework is crucial to understanding the role of governance in shaping the adoption of green initiatives within the maritime sector of the UAE. This theory posited that government policies and regulations play a central role in impacting the behaviour of companies and industries through the creation of incentives, the formation of standards, and the enforcement of compliance. It is observed that government intervention by the use of environmental policies played a contribution in driving the adoption of environmentally friendly practices in the maritime industry of UAE (Farrukh et al., 2023). The research has accentuated the importance of policy instruments that include regulations, economic incentives, and voluntary programs for fostering environmental sustainability. In the UAE, the government has demonstrated a commitment to sustainable maritime practices through the inclusion of policies that incentivize and regulate the adoption of green initiatives. For example, the National Climate Change Plan of UAE has delineated specific targets to reduce carbon emissions that provide a clear policy framework for the maritime sector to be in line with global efforts to combat climate change (Diaz et al., 2023). A key policy intervention that is suggested is the promotion of solar power in the maritime industry. The UAE government has implemented initiatives that offer financial incentives, tax breaks, and subsidies to companies that help to adopt solar energy solutions. This policy is in alignment with the theory as these measures create economic incentives for companies in the maritime sector to transition to renewable energy sources that reduce their reliance on fossil fuels and contribute to a more sustainable energy landscape. Furthermore, international environmental standards and regulations also help in the decision-making process of UAE companies and ports. The UAE as a key player in global trade and maritime activities has recognized the importance of adhering to international norms. An international framework is the International Maritime Organisation (IMO), which has set stringent regulations to address environmental challenges in the shipping industry (Garcia et al., 2021). These aspects include guidelines on emissions and the use of sustainable propulsion systems. The conformity of the UAE with these international standards reflects the influence of global environmental governance on the country's maritime policies. Practically, the UAE's adherence to international regulations is evident in the implementation of measures like the use of propulsion systems (Mneimneh et al., 2023). The UAE's commitment to comply with these standards not only reflects a proactive approach to environmental stewardship but has also positioned the country as a responsible global player in maritime sustainability. This theory has also emphasised the role of regulatory enforcement to ensure compliance with environmental standards by strict regulations governing vessel design and maintenance practices within the UAE, which prompts maritime operations and their alignment with sustainable principles. Henceforth, this theory is a comprehensive lens to analyse the impact of government policies and international regulations on the adoption of green initiatives within the UAE's maritime sector that helps to understand the proactive role of the UAE in being energy-efficient.

1.7.Nature of the Study

The nature of this study is fundamentally quantitative and aims to empirically investigate the extent of the adoption of environmentally friendly practices within the UAE's maritime industry. It also objectifies the corresponding impact on both efficiency and the health of the marine environment. The research question of this study delves into the specific practices of solar power, wind energy, innovative propulsion systems, and optimised vessel design and maintenance that seek to understand the degree of their embrace by UAE ports and shipping companies. The hypotheses framed around this question presents a binary exploration i.e., either there is no significant adoption or impact, as posited in the null hypothesis or there is practical embracement and a positive significant impact as implied in the alternative hypothesis. To test the hypothesis and evaluate the research question, a quantitative approach is aligned with the need for numerical data to quantify the level of adoption and measure the impact of green initiatives. The research has conducted surveys among UAE ports and shipping companies that enable the collection of structured, quantitative data that provide insights into the current practices and attitudes towards environmentally friendly initiatives. The inclusion of variables in the research is related to solar power, wind energy, innovative propulsion systems, and vessel design and maintenance that allows for a nuanced analysis of each aspect that contributes to a comprehensive understanding of the environmental sustainability landscape within the maritime sector. In this research, the statistical tools are applied by the use of t-tests and ANOVA variance, which is a strategic method to rigorously test the hypotheses. These tests aid in assessing the validity of the research. They also provide insights that contribute to forming an understanding of green shipping practices within the maritime sector. Prior to conducting the quantitative analysis, a thorough literature review is conducted that grounds the study in existing knowledge, identifies the gaps, and informs the development of the survey instrument. The literature review is composed of relevant studies on sustainable practices in the maritime industry that emphasise the research conducted in the context of the UAE and other regions that face similar challenges. Therefore, this study adopts a quantitative nature that employs surveys and statistical analyses, which helps in the systematic adoption and acceptance of environmentally friendly practices by UAE ports and shipping companies. This approach facilitates the evaluation of their impact on both operational efficiency and the overall health of the marine environment.

1.8. Definitions

The keywords of this paper include environmentally friendly practices, solar power, wind energy, innovative propulsion systems, optimised vessel design, UAE ports, shipping companies, the health of the marine environment, sustainable maritime practices, green initiatives, environmental impact, maritime industry, and global trade. Each of the key terms is defined below.

Table 1.

Definitions of Keywords

Keyword	Definitions
Environmentally friendly practices	These refer to actions and strategies implemented by organisations to minimise negative impacts on the environment that emphasise sustainability and ecological responsibility in various operational aspects (de la Peña Zarzuelo et al., 2020).
Solar power	Solar power involves the use of energy from the sun to generate electricity or heat (Nwaigwe et al., 2019).
Wind energy	Wind energy is the conversion of wind motion into mechanical or electrical energy (Chaudhuri et al., 2022).
Innovative propulsion systems	These are advanced technologies and mechanisms that are utilized to propel vessels where the focus is to reduce the environmental impact (Belibassakis et al., 2021).
Optimised vessel design	Optimised vessel design involves the creation of ships with enhanced efficiency, reduced environmental impact, and improved performance (Nuchturee et al., 2020).
UAE ports	The ports at UAE are at the trade hub and the most common ones are Abu Dhabi port, Ajman, Musaffah port, Al Hamriya port, and Fujairah port (Akhavan, 2019).
Shipping companies	Shipping companies are entities, which are involved in the transportation of goods and passengers based on maritime routes (Rachmawati et al., 2021).
Sustainable maritime practices	These are practices that prioritize long-term environmental, social, and economic viability in maritime operations that are aligned with principles of sustainability (Benamara et al., 2019).
Green initiatives	Green initiatives are actions and projects aimed at promoting environmental sustainability and reducing ecological impact that often involve the implementation of renewable energy sources and eco-friendly technologies (de Kat & Mouawad, 2019).
Maritime industry	The maritime industry includes all activities related to the transport of goods and passengers via water including shipping, ports, and associated services (Kechagias et al., 2022).
Global Trade	Global trade refers to the exchange of goods and services across international borders that involve economic transactions between countries and regions (Narlikar, 2021).

These definitions provide clarity on the selected keywords, contributing to an understanding of the literature keyword strategy. Additionally, they elucidate the rationale behind choosing the specific keyword for analysis.

1.9. Assumptions

There are several assumptions required for this research. These assumptions provide a foundational framework for the design, execution, and interpretation of the findings of the study. Firstly, it is assumed that the survey respondents from UAE ports and shipping companies have provided accurate and reliable information regarding the adoption of environmentally friendly practices. This assumption relies on the respondents' willingness to openly share details about their operational strategies that include the integration of solar power, wind energy, innovative propulsion systems, and optimised vessel design and maintenance. The assumption further assumes that the survey participants possess sufficient knowledge and awareness of the environmental initiatives of the organisation to provide meaningful insights. Additionally, an assumption is made that the responses of respondents reflect the actual state of green initiatives within their respective organisations that minimising the potential biases or inaccuracies in self-reporting. Another fundamental assumption is that the survey instrument effectively captures the nuances of environmentally friendly practices within the maritime industry. In this regard, the survey questions are designed to include key aspects like the extent of adoption, perceived efficiency gains, and observed influences on the health of the marine environment. It is also assumed that the chosen survey metrics are aligned with the research question allowing for a comprehensive analysis of the specified environmentally friendly practices. The assumption further posits that the survey instrument is clear, unbiased, and capable of eliciting meaningful responses from a diverse range of participants within the maritime sector. In terms of statistical analysis, the research has assumed that the chosen quantitative methods are appropriate for testing the hypotheses. The application of statistical techniques in this study assumes their appropriateness for comparing means. These tests serve to assess variations among distinct groups, offering robust insights into the levels of adoption and impact of green initiatives. Essential assumptions governing these tests involve the normal distribution of data and the homogeneity of variances, critical factors ensuring the validity of the statistical analyses. These foundational assumptions, in turn, boost the reliability of the quantitative results, aligning them with the research question. Additionally, the research presupposes that the literature review comprehensively addresses the implementation of green initiatives, effectively capturing insights associated with sustainable maritime practices in the UAE. This assumption is based on the thoroughness of the review process that includes the identification of relevant scholarly works, theoretical frameworks, and empirical studies. The literature review is expected to contribute foundational knowledge, guide the development of the survey instrument, and inform the interpretation of quantitative findings. It is assumed that the selected literature provides a comprehensive understanding of the current state of environmentally friendly practices in the maritime industry offering valuable insights into potential factors. The research has also assumed that the adoption of green initiatives within the UAE's maritime sector is influenced by a combination of internal organisational factors, external regulatory pressures, and global sustainability trends. This assumption has recognized the complexity of decision-making processes within companies and ports while acknowledging that multiple factors can contribute to or hinder the embracement of environmentally friendly practices. Hence, the research operates under the assumptions that survey respondents provide accurate and transparent information, the survey instrument effectively captures relevant dimensions of green initiatives, chosen statistical methods are suitable for hypothesis testing, the literature review comprehensively informs the study, and the adoption of environmentally friendly practices is influenced by a diverse array of internal and external factors within the maritime industry of UAE.

1.10   Scope and Delimitations

The scope of this research is composed of an in-depth examination of the adoption and impact of environmentally friendly practices within the maritime industry of UAE. The study is focused on the practices of solar power, wind energy, innovative propulsion systems, and optimised vessel design and maintenance within UAE ports and shipping companies. The temporal scope of the research is delimited to the current state of practices that provide a snapshot of the environmental initiatives of the industry at the time of data collection. The geographical scope is limited to the UAE which acknowledges the unique context of the nation's maritime industry and its strategic importance in global trade. The research aims to capture a comprehensive understanding of the extent to which these green initiatives are embraced by maritime entities in the UAE that elucidates on the interplay between sustainability efforts, operational efficiency, and the health of the marine environment.

The delimitations of this research are important to define the boundaries and constraints within which the study operates. Firstly, the study is delimited to the specific environmentally friendly practices mentioned in the research question. Though these practices are integral to sustainable maritime operations, other potential green initiatives can exist but are not within the purview of this research. Additionally, the research is delimited to quantitative analysis that relies on survey data and statistical methods like t-tests and ANOVA variance. In this case, qualitative methods like interviews or case studies are intentionally excluded from the scope due to the focused nature of the research question and the need for numerical data to test hypotheses. The study is further delimited to the perceptions and experiences of stakeholders within UAE ports and shipping companies as it can be biased. Though these stakeholder entities play a central role in the maritime sector, perspectives from other stakeholders like governmental bodies, environmental organisations, or international entities are not explored in this research. This delimitation ensures a targeted investigation into the specific actors that directly involves the adoption and impact of green initiatives within the maritime industry. Furthermore, the research does not delve into the economic implications or financial aspects of adopting environmentally friendly practices in detail. In this case, though the study acknowledges the economic dimension as a potential factor, a detailed economic analysis that includes cost-benefit assessments is beyond the scope of this research. Thus, the focus primarily sustains the environmental and operational aspects where economic considerations serve as contextual factors. Lastly, it is important to know that research does not extend to prescriptive recommendations or interventions to improve sustainable practices. These findings inform potential areas for improvement as the scope of the study is limited to descriptive and explanatory analyses that offer insights into the current state of affairs instead of proposition for specific actions among industry stakeholders. Therefore, the research scope is limited to examining the adoption and impact of particular environmentally friendly practices within the UAE's maritime industry. The study employs a quantitative analysis and specifically concentrates on the perceptions of stakeholders within UAE ports and shipping companies. These defined boundaries are set to ensure a rigorous investigation into the identified facets of sustainable green practices.

1.11. Limitations

A few limitations are inherent in this research the first one is that the study relies on self-reported data from survey respondents within UAE ports and shipping companies that introduce the possibility of response bias or social desirability bias. The accuracy of the information provided is contingent upon the willingness of respondents to disclose accurate details about their environmental practices. Additionally, the cross-sectional design of the research is limited in its ability to capture dynamic changes over time. The study is a provision of a snapshot of the current state of environmentally friendly practices, but it does not provide insights into the evolution of these practices along with a historical framework. Furthermore, the research has a focus exclusively on quantitative analysis that overlooks the rich contextual insights that qualitative methods could offer. The narrow economic scope has put a limit on the exploration of the financial implications of adopting green initiatives. Hence, these limitations underscore the need for cautious interpretation and acknowledgment of the study's constraints to shape the conclusions drawn from the findings.

1.12. Significance of the Study

This research holds immense significance on various fronts. Firstly, the research has addressed a critical gap in understanding the current state of environmentally friendly practices within the maritime industry of the UAE. Due to the escalating global concern for climate change and the specific vulnerabilities of UAE ports to rising sea levels, the study has contributed valuable insights into the extent of adoption of sustainable initiatives. Hence, through circumscribing solar power, wind energy, innovative propulsion systems, and optimised vessel design and maintenance, the research has offered a nuanced exploration of the industry's commitment to ecological responsibility and energy efficiency. Moreover, the study's findings have practical implications for policymakers, industry leaders, and stakeholders within the maritime sector of the UAE. Since the government and companies endeavor to align with international environmental standards and meet ambitious reduction targets, it is essential to understand the current landscape of green initiatives becomes paramount. Furthermore, the research has provided evidence-based insights that can inform strategic decision-making, guide policy formulations, and identify areas for targeted support and incentivization. Another significance of the research is extended beyond the broader global context of sustainable maritime practices. The UAE along with its strategic geographic location and bustling ports has served as a microcosm of the challenges faced by maritime hubs worldwide. The research findings contribute to the global discourse on the feasibility and impact of the integration of renewable energy sources and eco-friendly technologies into maritime operations. In this case, the information learned from the UAE experience can potentially inform best practices and inspire similar initiatives in other regions to grapple with the environmental consequences of maritime activities. Furthermore, the study is focused on quantitative analysis that includes statistical methods that add rigor to the exploration of adoption levels and impacts. The empirical evidence that is gathered through these analyses enhances the credibility of the findings and acts as a solid foundation for evidence-based decision-making. Henceforth, the significance of this study lies in its contribution to filling a knowledge gap, informing strategic decisions within the UAE's maritime industry, offering insights for global discussions on sustainable practices, and providing a methodologically robust examination of the adoption and impact of environmentally friendly green initiatives in the wake of rising environmental concerns and evolved international standards.

1.13. Theoretical Significance

Three theories—innovation diffusion, sustainable development, and environmental policy—are chosen. Although all of them meet the research criteria, the conceptual framework primarily aligns with the innovation diffusion theory. This theory provides a lens to understand the adoption patterns of environmentally friendly practices within the UAE's maritime industry. This theory is about innovations like sustainable technologies and practices that diffuse through a social system over time. Through the employment of this theoretical framework, the research aims to unravel the factors that affect the rate and extent of adoption of solar power, wind energy, innovative propulsion systems, and optimised vessel design and maintenance within the maritime sector of the UAE. It is important to understand how these innovations diffuse among UAE ports and how shipping companies offer theoretical insights into the dynamics of organisational decision-making along with the role of external influences, fostering a deeper comprehension of the pathways that permeate the industry. Keeping this information under consideration, the practical significance is also discussed that explicate about the tangible implications of the research findings for industry practitioners, policymakers, and stakeholders. It elucidates how the identified adoption patterns and impacts of green initiatives can inform practical strategies within the UAE's maritime sector. The practical significance is an exploration of how the evidence-based insights derived from the study can guide the formulation of targeted policies, investment decisions, and operational practices. The goal aimed through this practical guidance is to bridge the gap between theoretical understanding and actionable outcomes to enhance the sustainability of maritime operations in the UAE. Simultaneously, the significance for social change lies in the broader societal implications of the research. It delves into how the study contributes to the larger narrative, fostering environmental responsibility within the maritime industry. The research is about the potential social changes that can emanate from a concerted effort toward ecological responsibility through the extent to which UAE ports and shipping companies embrace sustainable practices. Hence, the following is an exploration of how the industry's commitment to green initiatives can catalyze practical and positive social change that influences public perceptions, and contributes to a broader global shift.

1.13.1. Practical Significance

The practical significance of this research is paramount and offers tangible implications for industry practitioners, policymakers, and stakeholders within the maritime sector of the UAE. The findings derived from the study are framed within the theoretical lens of innovation diffusion that carries substantial weight to guide practical strategies to enhance the sustainability of maritime operations. For industry practitioners, the research acts as a compass that provides nuanced insights into the current state of adoption of environmentally friendly practices. The research aids in assessing the prevailing patterns and factors that influence the use of green initiatives to inform operational decisions. The companies within the maritime sector can use these insights to benchmark their practices that identify areas for improvement and strategically align with global trends in sustainable maritime operations. From a policy perspective, the practical significance of the research lies in its capacity to create targeted and effective interventions. For this purpose, policymakers can leverage the evidence-based findings to craft regulations and incentives that align with the current dynamics of the industry. In this context, the research provides a foundation for the formulation of policies that not only promote the adoption of green initiatives but also address specific challenges and barriers associated in the UAE's maritime industry. Policymakers need to tailor their approaches based on the nuanced understanding of how innovations diffuse within the industry that fosters an environment conducive to the accelerated adoption of sustainable practices. Moreover, the practical significance extends to the realm of investment decisions where industry stakeholders like government bodies and private investors can utilize the research findings to strategically allocate resources. The identification of prevalent environmentally friendly practices and their impact on efficiency along with the marine environment helps in informing investment decisions in technologies and infrastructure. The green practices allow stakeholders to prioritize funding towards initiatives that have demonstrated efficacy for both enhanced operational efficiency and minimised environmental impact. This strategic allocation of resources contributes to the long-term sustainability of maritime operations that is aligned with financial investments and ecological responsibility. Furthermore, the research's practical significance is evident in its potential to catalyze collaborative initiatives within the industry as the insights derived from the study serve as a common ground for fostering collaboration among maritime companies, industry associations, and governmental bodies (Bax et al., 2022). The stakeholders of research can leverage the findings to engage in knowledge-sharing, best practices, and collaborative efforts that are aimed at the collective advancement of the sustainability agenda. This collaborative approach not only enhances the practical implementation of green initiatives but also adopts a culture of shared responsibility and commitment to environmental stewardship within the maritime community. Hence, the practical significance of this research lies in its capacity to guide industry practices, inform policymaking, drive strategic investments, and foster collaborative efforts toward a more sustainable future for the maritime sector of the UAE.

1.13.2. Significance to Social Change

The significance of the social change that stems from this research is profound since it illuminates the transformative potential of green practices within the maritime industry of the UAE. Based on the theoretical perspective's conceptual framework, the research findings hold the promise to catalyze positive societal shifts toward greater environmental responsibility. One aspect of this social change is reflected in the potential influence in terms of public perceptions and awareness. Since the UAE's maritime industry embraces and implements sustainable practices, it habecome a beacon for public discourse on the nexus between commerce and ecological stewardship (Spiegel-Feld et al., 2023). The findings present a narrative that extends beyond industry boundaries, permeating public consciousness and shaping society's perspective on the role of maritime operations in the broader context of environmental sustainability. Moreover, the significance of research to social change extends to its potential impact on consumer behaviour since consumers become increasingly environmentally conscious about the practices adopted by the maritime industry that can shape consumer choices and preferences (Kardzhilov, 2023). The research findings explain that conscious consumers adopt solar power, wind energy, innovative propulsion systems, and optimised vessel design and maintenance as they are aware of the negative impact on the environment and want to make sustainable changes to ensure adaptability. In turn, the demand is driven for products and services associated with environmentally responsible maritime practices that create a positive feedback loop where industry practices and consumer choices mutually reinforce each other in favor of sustainability. Additionally, the research holds the potential to influence educational and awareness initiatives related to maritime sustainability. The findings of the research can serve as a foundational resource for educational programs, both within academic institutions and public outreach efforts. The research makes use of successful cases of green initiatives that have positive impacts in terms of interconnectedness between the maritime industry and environmental health. This knowledge disseminates a culture of environmental literacy that empowers individuals to make informed decisions and advocate for sustainable practices within their communities. Furthermore, the significance of social change is evident in the potential emulation effect on other industries and regions as the UAE's maritime industry leads the way in the adoption of green initiatives that become a model for emulation by other sectors and nations that counter similar challenges (Gisle, 2023). The research findings serve as a blueprint to demonstrate the feasibility and benefits of incorporating sustainable technologies and practices within industrial operations. This ripple effect can contribute to a global shift towards environmentally responsible practices in maritime trade that inspire collaborative efforts across borders and industries to address shared environmental challenges. Hence, the significance of research to social change lies in its potential to shape public perceptions, influence consumer behaviour, contribute to educational initiatives, and inspire emulation by other industries and regions through positive societal effects.

1.14. Summary and Transition

This chapter has set a foundation for the research paper, it has clearly explained the background of the research along with the problem statement and purpose of the study. The research has also established the research questions and hypotheses to be investigated along with the theoretical background. Three theoretical foundations that are elucidated in the chapter are innovation diffusion, sustainable development, and environment policy. Moreover, the nature of the study along with its scope, delimitations, limitations, and significance are also discussed. The upcoming chapter involves a comprehensive literature review, where scholarly databases are utilized to review and assess relevant literature. This review aims to understand the theoretical foundation, conceptual framework, and key themes that pertain to the topic. Lastly, the chapter explains the research gap that helps to move towards research methodology and primary research.

Chapter 2

LITERATURE REVIEW

The literature review is gathered through scholarly articles that are available on Google Scholar. The review is composed of the historical background of the research topic, theoretical findings of the research, and elucidation of conceptual analysis in a practical context. Furthermore, case studies are also discussed to conduct the review thoroughly and develop a key insight on the topic.

The review is based on the collection of credible sources on the topic of "green practices at UAE ports and companies for maritime energy management" that imposes a structured approach. The steps for the research that are implemented are discussed here. Firstly, the research objectives are established that help in setting the line for the literature review and its themes. The second step is the need to identify the keywords that are already mentioned in Table 1 of definitions. This technique sorts the keywords such as "green shipping", "UAE ports", "maritime energy management", "maritime industry", and "environment sustainability practices". These keywords help in finding relevant sources from online databases. For this purpose, academic journals and databases are utilized to inquire about energy management practices by UAE ports and companies. The information found in these articles is reviewed based on themes in the subsequent sections. Furthermore, the strategy to search on the browser i.e., Boolean search on Google Scholar is also highlighted in the next section before conducting the review for historical background i.e., the evaluation of the changes at UAE ports over time. After the establishment of history, the literature search strategy i.e., Boolean search is chosen where operators like OR, AND, and NOT are used to find the articles that suit the title of the research. Furthermore, the inclusion criteria are also set where recent articles since 2019 are selected (Gras, 2013). For this purpose, a filter is applied to Google Scholar to scrutinize the articles. During the research, the unrelated and inefficient sources are excluded. Once the articles are scrutinized, the articles that are available in full text are selected for the conduction of a detailed review that assesses the relevance, findings, and techniques used in the research. This helps in knowing about the quality of the research along with explaining the feasibility of the research design. The review is about the theoretical frameworks chosen i.e., innovation diffusion theory, sustainable development theory, and environment policy theory along with other practical aspects. This explicates the maritime industry and green shipping practices that are implemented and can be endorsed. The findings are sorted in the form of themes that help to understand the categorical, practical, and theoretical findings. Finally, the review also summarizes the case studies that are real-time scenarios of green shipping initiatives at UAE ports that help to analyse the challenges countered and implement strategies (Bloomfield & Fisher, 2019). All these findings ultimately lead to finding the research gap in the existing literature that helps in conducting primary analysis and forming a survey. Hence, the literature review is a systematic one where different actions are taken in a stepwise manner to gather information on the research topic and set the foundation for the research question.

2.1. Historical Literature

The maritime industry in UAE has a rich and diverse history that spans over centuries, has witnessed transformative changes, and has become a vital hub for global trade. For this purpose, historical analysis and assessment are done for the past years that have revealed distinct phases of the evolution of the UAE's maritime industry.

The first phase of the historical evolution of the UAE port is an ancient maritime connection in the pre-Islamic era. According to the findings of Lidour and Beech (2020), the coastal regions of the Arabian Peninsula in the present-day UAE have a long history of maritime activities, which dates back to ancient times. The archaeological evidence from research implicates that even before the Islamic era, the inhabitants of the region engaged in seafaring and maritime trade. The proximity to the Arabian Sea and the Persian Gulf has facilitated trade connections with neighboring civilizations of the Mesopotamians and the Indus Valley creating a maritime network that laid the foundation for future trade routes.

The second phase is of Islamic maritime trade from the 7th to 15th century since the advent of Islam in the 7th century when maritime trade gained further significance. According to the findings of Meicun (2022), the coastal areas of the UAE became integral to the broader Islamic maritime trade network that connects the Arabian Peninsula with regions across Asia and Africa. The rise of Islamic empires like the Abbasids and later the Ottomans have contributed to the flourishing trade routes. During this period, the maritime industry in the UAE saw the development of active ports along with the establishment of maritime trade routes that played a key role in the global movement of goods.

The third phase is of Portuguese and European exploration from the 15th to 18th century where the 15th century witnessed a significant shift in the global maritime landscape with the age of exploration (Power, 2024). Portuguese explorers who sought new trade routes to Asia had ventured into the Indian Ocean and the Persian Gulf. The strategic location of the UAE's coastline made it a focal point for European maritime activities. At this time, the Portuguese established control over key ports in the region including Hormuz that influenced trade dynamics (Power, 2024). However, their dominance was later challenged by other European powers including the Dutch and the British which led to geopolitical changes that shaped the maritime landscape.

The fourth phase is the influence of the British and the decline of maritime trade during the 19th century which marked changes in the Gulf region especially in UAE. According to Ketbi (2020), the British have established treaties with local rulers to secure maritime routes and protect their imperial interests. However, the decline of traditional maritime trade routes and the emergence of steamships and the Suez Canal resulted in a shift in global trade dynamics. Hence, the decline of traditional show-based trade signalled a challenging period for the UAE's maritime industry.

The fifth phase is of oil boom and modernization during the 20th century as oil was discovered in UAE and it led to a profound transformation in the country's economy and, consequently in the maritime industry (Al Jaberi, 2019). The newfound wealth had allowed substantial investments in infrastructure in the 20th century that included the development of modern ports. Ports like Jebel Ali had emerged as important hubs for the export of oil and the import of goods (Akhavan, 2020). Hence, the modernization of the maritime industry was characterized by the introduction of advanced technologies that increased the capacity for accommodating the growing demands of global trade.

The last phase is diversification and sustainability which is marked from the late 20th century to the present. In the last few decades, the UAE has undertaken significant efforts to diversify its economy and reduce dependency on oil. This diversification has extended to the maritime industry where the focus is on sustainability. During the 21st century, the world has seen the implementation of environmentally friendly practices in response to global concerns about climate change (Shadab, 2019). In this regard, initiatives such as the adoption of renewable energy sources, innovative propulsion systems, and optimised vessel design show the UAE's commitment to sustainable maritime operations.

Henceforth, the historical analysis of the UAE's maritime industry has revealed a dynamic evolution that is shaped by ancient trade connections, Islamic maritime trade, European exploration, British influence, the oil boom, and a modernization drive. The industry has continuously adapted to the changed global dynamics, and in the contemporary era, the UAE has embraced sustainability as a key focus. Thus, the historical trajectory has provided valuable insights into the resilience and adaptability of the UAE's maritime sector.

2.2. Literature Search Strategy

To create a literature review, there is a need to implement a strategy, and for this research, the strategy of Boolean search is chosen i.e., the use of operators like AND and OR to make search queries (Scells et al., 2020). In this regard, efficient use of research keywords is required based on keyword strategy to test the hypothesis by the use of accurate research (Mengist et al., 2020). Based on this strategy, the following table exhibits the search key terms and search queries used for the literature review.

Table 2.

Search Queries-based Boolean Operators

Operator	Keyword	Combinations
AND, OR	Environmentally friendly practices, UAE ports, shipping companies	"Environmentally friendly practices" AND "UAE ports" OR "Shipping companies" AND "Marine environment"
AND, OR	Solar power, UAE ports, shipping companies, marine environment	"Solar power" AND "UAE ports" OR "Shipping companies" AND "Marine environment"
AND, OR	Wind energy, UAE ports, shipping companies, marine environment	"Wind energy" AND "UAE ports" OR "Shipping companies" AND "Marine environment"
AND, OR	Innovative propulsion systems, UAE ports, shipping companies, marine environment	"Innovative propulsion systems" AND "UAE ports" OR "Shipping companies" AND "Marine environment"
AND, OR	Optimised vessel design, UAE ports, shipping	"Optimised vessel design" AND "UAE ports" OR "Shipping companies" AND "Marine environment"

	companies, marine environment	
AND	Sustainable maritime practices, UAE ports, shipping companies, marine environment	"Sustainable maritime practices" AND "UAE ports" AND "Shipping companies" AND "Marine environment"
AND	Green initiatives, UAE ports, shipping companies, marine environment	"Green initiatives" AND "UAE ports" AND "Shipping companies" AND "Marine environment"
Case studies	Green shipping practices case studies, UAE ports	"CASE STUDIES on green practices in UAE ports"
AND	Global trade, UAE ports, shipping companies, marine environment	"Global Trade" AND "UAE ports" AND "Shipping companies" AND "Marine environment"

Searching these queries sort the search and provide only relevant research articles for review. Each of these search terms has provided a list of articles that are chosen for further analysis in the next sections.

2.3. Theoretical Foundation

The main three theories that are the advocates of this topic are innovation diffusion theory, sustainable development theory, and environment policy theory. To explore the theoretical foundation, each of the theories is elucidated in the context of UAE ports of the maritime industry.

There is a diverse pool of articles that provide valuable insights into the challenges and opportunities related to sustainable practices and technology adoption within the maritime industry. However, a few articles that are aligned with the theoretical framework of innovation diffusion theory are explicated. According to Chua and colleagues (2023), sustainable shipping management contributes to the understanding of the critical success factors (CSFs) along with drivers that influence the adoption of sustainable practices in the maritime sector. Applying the innovation diffusion theory to the findings, a key notion is developed: the factors influencing the diffusion of sustainable practices encompass government support, organisational commitment, and technology acceptance. The theory allowed conceptualizing the process by which these factors diffuse across the maritime industry that affects organisational performance. Moreover, the study has acknowledged the contingent nature of the relationships that underscore the importance of internal and external conditions that are aligned with the core principles of the theory. Another article by Somorin and colleagues (2019) has focused on clean energy technologies in developing countries since it provides insights relevant to the diffusion of innovation in the maritime sector. The challenges of the industry have highlighted questions on the availability, accessibility, and appropriateness of clean energy technologies that resonate with the concerns often faced by the maritime industry to adopt sustainable practices. This theory can be applied to understand the factors that influence the adoption of clean energy technologies in the maritime context through consideration of issues of reliability and affordability. Furthermore, the article has discussed case studies that offer practical examples of the diffusion process in diverse African countries that contribute to the theoretical understanding of innovation dissemination in different contexts (Somorin et al., 2019). The adoption of technology in African countries varies across different sectors and regions, and there has been a noticeable and growing trend of technology adoption in various domains. Firstly, African countries have experienced a rapid increase in mobile phone usage and mobile technology adoption where mobile phones have become a ubiquitous tool for communication along with banking and financial transactions. Secondly, several African countries have seen significant advancements in financial technology (fintech) such that mobile money platforms and digital payment solutions have gained popularity. This use of technology provides convenient and accessible financial services to a large portion of the population. Moreover, some African governments have implemented e-government initiatives to improve the efficiency and transparency of public services, which include online platforms for citizen engagement, electronic tax systems, and digital public administration services. Furthermore, to address energy challenges, some African countries are adopting innovative technologies for renewable energy. These changes manifest that technology acceptance is done easily through proper efforts by the government and all the key stakeholders. While progress has been made, challenges such as limited infrastructure, connectivity issues, and resource constraints continue to impact the pace of technology adoption in some regions. Additionally, efforts are being made to bridge the digital divide and ensure that the benefits of technology reach a broader segment of the population. Lastly, the findings by Ikpogu (2021) are framed within Yang and Lin's (2023) concept of maritime shipping digitization and the concept of technology acceptance. This research has explored the barriers to technology adoption in the maritime industry where the theory is particularly relevant to analyse the resistance and slow acceptance of new technologies among stakeholders. The research has identified technology adoption standards, barriers to digitization along with factors that impact technology acceptance, and the resources needed for adoption within the maritime sector. These themes are aligned with the stages of innovation diffusion that provide a lens that helps to interpret the challenges faced by the maritime industry to embrace technological advancements. These pieces of research collectively contribute to the literature on sustainable practices and technology adoption within the maritime industry that offers theoretical insights. Therefore, this theoretical foundation enhances the comprehension of the complexities associated with the adoption of environmentally friendly practices and technology in the maritime industry that underscore the need for tailored strategies and interventions for facilitating successful diffusion and integration.

The second theory is the sustainable development theory, which explores the topic and befits the concept of maritime sustainability. According to the findings of Lam and Li (2019), this theory has emphasised the prominence of balancing economic prosperity, social well-being, and environmental quality in port operations. The focus on green marketing has reflected a commitment to sustainable development as the ports aim to attract customers who prioritize sustainability. The study has explored green marketing strategies, structures, and functions among major ports around the globe that resonate with the core tenets of the theoretical framework. The findings of the research have suggested a positive trend with more than half of the major ports actively engaged in green marketing, though there is room for improvement to integrate strategies, structures, and functions for a holistic sustainable approach. Another research by Wang and colleagues (2020) has provided a comprehensive overview of the maritime industry's role to contribute to the UN's Sustainable Development Goals (SDGs). The theory posited that economic, environmental, and social aspects are interconnected as they explore how the maritime industry engages with each SDG. Through the application of the concept of social entrepreneurship, the study has categorized the industry's responsibilities that identify potential collaborations within the value chain. The unified framework proposed by the research is aligned with the theory that emphasises the varied motives and levels of comprehensiveness in the maritime industry's sustainability efforts. Thus, this framework not only contributes to theoretical understanding but also offers managerial insinuations for resource allocation strategies for meeting SDGs. The last article reviewed for this theoretical perspective is by Parmentola and colleagues (2022) which explains the role of blockchain technology in environmental sustainability. The article has investigated whether blockchain can contribute to achieving sustainable development goals to improve supply chain sustainability, enhance energy efficiency, and support the development of smart cities. These findings articulate the findings of the potential positive impacts of blockchain on environmental sustainability that are aligned with the interconnected goals of economic, environmental, and social development. However, the research has also acknowledged potential negative effects that need consideration. One notable concern is the energy consumption associated with certain blockchain networks, especially those that utilize proof-of-work consensus mechanisms. The energy-intensive mining process in these networks has raised environmental sustainability questions that contribute to the environment. Additionally, the electronic waste generated from the constant need for hardware upgrades in mining operations poses a challenge to responsible e-waste management. Moreover, the decentralized and pseudonymous nature of blockchain transactions raises regulatory and ethical considerations, as it may facilitate illicit activities or hinder accountability in certain cases. Addressing these negative aspects is important to maximise the benefits of blockchain technology for sustainable development. This article is an essential contribution to the theoretical understanding of how technological innovations such as blockchain can align with theory to address global challenges. Hence, these findings collectively reinforce the relevance of theory to understand and guide practices within the maritime industry that showcase how major ports, the maritime industry, and emerging technologies are actively engaged with the principles of sustainable development based on economic viability.

The final theory applied to this topic is the environmental policy theory, as evidenced by Li and colleagues' (2023) focus on the integrated governance of port clusters in the Yangtze River Delta. This aligns with the principles and perspectives of the environmental policy theory. It has emphasised the need for coordinated efforts to enhance port efficiency and marine economic benefits. The article's findings have underscored the economic contribution, competitiveness, resource utilization, and sustainable development capability of Shanghai Port in comparison to Ningbo-Zhoushan Port. The research has recommended integrated governance, reasonable division of labor among ports, and government intervention in coastal management that is aligned with the principles of environmental policy. Hence, the article has emphasised the role of regulatory measures to promote sustainable practices within port clusters. Another article by Elnajjar and colleagues (2021) explored the environmental impact of seaport activities and introduced the concept of green ports that directly connect with the theory. The research has investigated the feasibility of applying renewable energy sources like wind and solar power to the Port of Jebel Ali as the study addressed the environmental concerns associated with port operations. The research findings have demonstrated cost reduction and lower energy costs through the integration of renewable energy that suggests practical solutions to mitigate the environmental impact of seaports. Thus, the article is aligned with the idea that environmental policies like the promotion of green practices and renewable energy adoption can positively influence the maritime industry, and they should be endorsed for the increased efficiency of UAE ports. Lastly, an article by Alblooshi and Ebrahim (2022) has framed this study that investigated the impact of port performances on economic development in various countries, specifically at UAE ports. Through the examination of components such as hinterland access, port and terminal efficiency, and port charges, this study aims to provide insights that can inform environmental policies related to port operations. The findings reveal that hinterland activities at the ports do not significantly impact economic development. This contributes to the understanding of how environmental policies may need to be tailored to specific aspects of port operations to achieve desired economic and environmental outcomes. Therefore, this study has compounded these three theories that help to develop the conceptual framework that has provided a guideline towards literature review.

2.4. Conceptual Framework

The conceptual framework of this research is on the sustainable practices that exist within the UAE maritime industry. The conceptual framework for this research is grounded in three key theoretical perspectives i.e., innovation diffusion theory, sustainable development theory, and environmental policy theory. These theories have provided a comprehensive lens for understanding the complexities associated with the adoption of environmentally friendly practices and technology in the maritime industry, especially UAE ports. At the core of the conceptual framework is innovation diffusion which helps to analyse the process through which sustainable practices and technologies are embraced within the maritime sector. The key investigative aspects of the study include sustainable shipping management, use of clean energy technologies, and maritime shipping digitization that adds key insights to the research. The theory allowed to identify critical success factors, drivers, and barriers that influence the diffusion of innovations within maritime sectors. In this regard, government support, organisational commitment, and technology acceptance emerge as key factors that affect the adoption of sustainable use of maritime practices and technologies (Vairetti et al., 2019). This theory is essential to understanding how these innovations spread across the maritime industry impact organisational performance and influence the decision-making process. There is a second stage of the conceptual framework as well, which sustainable development theory. Green marketing, maritime industry's role in SDGs, and role of blockchain technology in environment that contribute to energy management (Fraga-Lamas et al., 2020). This theory has guided the exploration of the interconnectedness of the economic, social, and environmental aspects of ports. The research has accentuated the importance of balanced, holistic approaches to achieve sustainable growth due to the integration of green marketing strategies, attainment of SDGs, and leveraging innovative technologies such as blockchain to foster sustainability within the maritime industry. Lastly, the theoretical framework of environment policy theory is a dimension that deals with integrated governance of port clusters and the investigation of the environmental impact of seaport activities align with this theory. This framework has postulated the role of coordinated governance efforts, regulatory measures, and interventions by the government to enhance port efficiency and ensure marine economic benefits. In this regard, the emphasis of research is aligned to industry practices with environmental policie that promote green ports and explore renewable energy applications to mitigate the ecological footprint of seaports. These three theories are interwoven for providing a comprehensive understanding of how innovations in sustainable practices diffuse, contribute to the broader goals of sustainable development, and meet the standard with environmental policies in the maritime industry of the UAE. This conceptual framework has considered the intricate relationships among the adoption of sustainable practices to maintain quality of environment and regulatory measures. Therefore, through integration of these theories, the research intends to develop a nuanced understanding of how UAE ports and shipping companies embrace environmentally friendly practices that impact efficiency and marine health along with the role of various factors that influence these processes.

2.5. Literature Review

The review is a detail of different articles that are selected from careful analysis that help to explore the topic. To avoid repetition of sources and incoherent research results, there is a need to consider various themes that help to set the tone of the research and develop a key notion on the topic i.e., maritime energy management at UAE ports.

2.5.1. Environment-Friendly Practices at UAE Ports

This theme of the review has elucidated the market entry strategies for healthy vegan chocolate to the challenges and opportunities presented by digital transformation in ports, helping to ensure sustainability. In this regard, sustainable facility management is integrated with green supply chain initiatives, UAE's strategic efforts in the food supply chain amid global changes, and the impact of green maritime transportation on emissions reduction through vertical alliances. All these aspects are relevant to environmental sustainability and its implications for the UAE, especially within the maritime industry. An article by Almeida (2023) has delved into the challenges of digital transformation in ports globally. The research has recognized the crucial role of digitalization in modernizing ports but also highlighted the unique challenges associated with the complexity of port operations. This is particularly relevant to the theme of environmentally friendly practices at UAE ports since digitalization is often a key driver in implementing sustainable practices. The findings of this study provide insights into the complexities that ports face in adopting environmentally friendly digital solutions to acknowledge that these innovations must align with operational intricacies and stakeholder demands. Another article by Formaneck (2019) has investigated the integration of Sustainable Facility Management (SFM) with Green Supply Chain Management (GSCM) initiatives in the UAE. These findings are aligned with the theme of environmentally friendly practices at UAE ports that help to explore how sustainable practices integrated into facility management and supply chain initiatives can contribute to the UAE's vision for sustainable development. Hence, the study acts as a baseline for green and environment-friendly initiatives that help to understand the eminence of green technologies at UAE ports. Another article by Salem and Jagadeesan (2022) has shifted the attention towards the UAE's strategic efforts in the food supply chain, particularly in the face of challenges posed by the pandemic, geopolitical shifts, and climate change. This research has explicated the broader supply chain dynamics that include transportation and logistics, which are integral components of the maritime industry. Hence, the emphasis on sustainable food security initiatives indirectly accentuates the need for environmentally friendly practices in the broader context of the supply chain. Finally, the article by C. Wang and Wang (2023) explored the impact of green maritime transportation on emissions reduction through vertical alliances between port and shipping enterprises. The findings of the article are aligned directly with the theme of environmentally friendly practices at UAE ports. It has delved into the strategies employed by ports and shipping companies to reduce emissions and enhance environmental performance. Thus, the study has emphasised the importance of vertical alliances as effective mechanisms to achieve sustainable goals in the maritime supply chain. All these articles have explicitly discussed environmentally friendly practices at UAE ports where the researchers have provided valuable insights into related aspects like market dynamics, digitalization challenges, sustainable facility management, supply chain sustainability, and emissions reduction strategies. Therefore, these indirect connections underscore the interconnected nature of sustainability considerations through various facets of the maritime industry in the UAE.

2.5.2. Solar Power at UAE Ports

There is an incessant need to collectively understand the utilization of solar energy at UAE ports that showcases diverse perspectives to harness renewable energy for sustainable port operations. In this regard, the findings of Joubi and colleagues (2022) are focused on hydrogen production from surplus solar electricity that presents a comprehensive model for solar hydrogen production and delivery in the UAE. The researchers have compared concentrated solar power (CSP) and photovoltaics (PV) that are being coupled with a solid oxide cell electrolyser since it is the most favourable pathway for large-scale hydrogen production. This piece of research has emphasised hydrogen as an energy carrier that underscored the potential for solar energy to not only power ports directly but also facilitate energy storage and export that are aligned with the UAE's commitment to sustainable energy practices (Joubi et al., 2022). Another article by Ramachandran and colleagues (2022) has emphasised the use of solar energy in the UAE as they have recognized the country's exceptional sun exposure rates, recent advances, electricity production, consumption, tariffs, and various key aspects of photovoltaic solar installation projects across different emirates. Thus, there is a need to endorse an appropriate use of solar energy projects within and outside the UAE that indicates a pivotal shift towards cleaner and more sustainable energy sources. Another article by Elnajjar and colleagues (2021) has taken a unique approach to address the environmental impact of seaport activities and propositions of green energy solutions that are especially focused on the Port of Jebel Ali. The research by a prototype experiment of UAE ports assesses the wind and solar potential where it demonstrates promising performances in terms of cost reduction and lower levelized cost of energy. This initiative is aligned with the broader theme of sustainable and environmentally friendly operation of seaports that showcases the feasibility of integrating renewable energy sources for mitigation of the environmental footprint of port activities. In the evolved macroeconomic landscape of UAE, the research by Salimi and colleagues (2022) has investigated the trend of solar energy production and consumption that acknowledges the country's economic reliance on oil and gas. The researchers have performed a SWOT analysis on different types of solar energy in the UAE that revealed promising strategies to transition towards renewable energy. Hence, the research has emphasised the strengths and opportunities of the strategies that could reduce fossil fuel demand, mitigate greenhouse gas emissions, and position the UAE as a leader in the carbon market of the Gulf Cooperation Council. Lastly, the article by Kandiyil (2022) has broadened the perspective through discussion on renewable energies as crucial components for achieving sustainability in ports. These energies include wind, solar, waves, tides, ocean thermal energy conversion, and salinity gradient. The research underscored that ports are vital to a nation's economy and they advocated to integrate renewable energy into ports' energy usage. Thus, the study has highlighted feasibility study, energy usage analysis, and site-specific device development as key steps to make renewable energy more accessible to the port community. All these articles collectively manifest the significant strides the UAE is making to adopt solar energy at its ports in the form of hydrogen production and storage to broader solar energy utilization trends along with specific initiatives at seaports of UAE.

2.5.3. Wind Energy at UAE Ports

Wind energy is used widely at UAE ports as a vital aspect of sustainable energy practices. Different research articles have reviewed valuable insights into the feasibility, challenges, and potential innovations in this domain. The research article by Fandi and colleagues (2022) underscored the UAE's commitment to renewable energy technologies that include wind to address the rising energy demand. Through acknowledgement of the investments in solar, nuclear, and other sources, the research has explicated the concept of tidal energy as a highly predictable and sustainable solution. The preliminary study implicates the installation of tidal lagoons integrated with reversible turbines at Saqar Port in Ras Al Khaimah and provides a glimpse into the potential to harness tidal energy to meet a significant portion of the UAE's energy demand. These findings are affirmed by Khan and Al Marashda (2023) who delved into the specific application of wind power in the UAE through the country's first wind farm project. The research highlighted challenges faced in offshore logistics to transport breakbulk cargo are addressed through the introduction of logistics barges that offer a cost-effective and efficient alternative. The research has provided an overview of the wind energy project executed in 2022 that provides insights into the challenges encountered and the lessons learned during its execution. Hence, the research has emphasised logistics solutions and the utilization of offshore wind energy that added to the broader understanding of implementing wind energy at UAE ports. Another article by Mahdy (2020) has broadened the perspective to encompass the entire Arabian Peninsula to propose a systematic assessment methodology for offshore wind energy potential. The methodology of the research in Egypt is based on an analytical hierarchy process and GIS that contributes to the country's renewable energy targets. The research has identified suitable high wind areas and estimated the offshore wind energy potential that provides a blueprint for the development of wind farms. Hence, the proposed methodology is hailed as globally applicable and offers a comprehensive framework to assess offshore wind energy suitability on both local and regional scales. Moreover, the article by Clemente and colleagues (2023) is focused on the integration of marine renewable sources to enhance the efficiency and sustainability of seaports. The research through analysis of the container-terminal case studies has identified smart seaports that excel in automation, real-time management, and energy efficiency. The potential integration with marine renewable-energy systems is considered that be aligned with the green energy transition at seaports. Hence, this holistic approach is aimed at constructing a model port that represents the expected evolution towards more sustainable and energy-efficient seaports globally. Lastly, the article by Alsubal and colleagues (2021) focused on Malaysia which contributes valuable insights into the life cycle cost analysis of an offshore wind farm in Kudat. The study has determined cost drivers and a breakdown of the whole life cycle cost structure that expounds on the economic aspects of offshore wind energy development. Thus, through a focus on the leveled cost of energy (LCOE), it is important to understand the economic viability of offshore wind projects. All these articles collectively contribute to the understanding of wind energy at UAE ports and beyond in terms of tidal energy feasibility to logistics solutions for offshore wind projects, systematic assessments of offshore wind energy potential, and the integration of marine renewable sources in global seaports.

2.5.4. Innovative propulsion systems at UAE Ports

The integration of innovative propulsion systems in seaports is an important step to achieve sustainability and comply with increasingly stringent environmental regulations. The research by Nguyen and colleagues (2021) has accentuated the challenges faced by ship designers to select and optimise propulsion architectures. The research has highlighted the imperative to reduce greenhouse gas emissions and adhere to the International Maritime Organisation's environmental standards. The initiation of electric propulsion systems has emerged as a transformative solution that offered benefits like improved compliance with international laws, enhanced flexibility, reduced operating costs, and access to advanced automation. The research has reviewed conventional and advanced electrical propulsion systems that presented a detailed comparison to aid ship owners and designers in optimising powertrain systems for commercial fleets. The research has further addressed strategies for sustainable maritime transport to emphasise the efficient use of renewable energy sources and electrical energy storage systems. In another article, Korberg and colleagues (2021) have adopted a forward-looking perspective to analyse the potential of renewable fuels in various propulsion systems for the maritime sector by 2030. In this regard, a fuel cost analysis is performed for biofuels, bio-electro fuels, electrofuels, liquid hydrogen, and electricity in different production pathways. The research has evaluated the total cost of ownership for different ship types through consideration of internal combustion engines, fuel cells, or battery-electric propulsion systems. The research findings have revealed that battery-electric propulsion is cost-competitive, especially for large ferries. In this regard, factors such as fuel cost, utilization rates, and propulsion types play a pivotal role in influencing the competitiveness of different fuels and propulsion systems. Another article by McCarney (2020) has delved into historical disruptive innovations in the maritime sector that draw parallels with the transition from wind power to carbon-based fuel power in the 19th century. The research has examined how the shipping sector managed disruptive change in the past by the use of technology options to reduce environmental impact and meet international requirements on ship emissions limits. The focus of the research is on the evolution of the engine room concerned with energy conversion and energy storage. Hence, this piece of research has provided valuable insights into potential pathways for the contemporary shipping industry to manage the impending decarbonization. Moreover, the article by K. Kim and colleagues (2020) has explained the use of a specific alternative fuel i.e., ammonia as a potential carbon-free fuel for ships. The research elaborates on the proposal of four propulsion systems for a 2500 Twenty-foot Equivalent Unit (TEU) container feeder ship, all of which are fueled by ammonia. The systems that include main engines are generators, polymer electrolyte membrane fuel cells (PEMFC), and solid oxide fuel cells (SOFC) that are compared from both economic and environmental perspectives. Hence, the research has revealed that ammonia can indeed be a carbon-free fuel for ships, with the SOFC power system identified as the most eco-friendly alternative regardless of a higher lifecycle cost. Lastly, the article by Jelić and colleagues (2021) has broadened the implementation of various environmental-friendly propulsion concepts that include the use of renewable energy sources. The research has provided a comprehensive review of potential solutions like environmental-friendly fuels in existing propulsion architecture, hybrid propulsion, and all-electric propulsion with renewable energy sources. The analysis of the findings has highlighted the advantages and disadvantages of each proposed solution that emphasised the challenges associated with limited energy storage capacity and the production and recycling of energy storage devices. Therefore, these articles have contributed to the understanding of the current landscape and future possibilities of innovative propulsion systems at seaports that promote the adoption of electric propulsion systems to the analysis of renewable fuels and the exploration of ammonia as a carbon-free option to create potential pathways for sustainable propulsion in the maritime industry.

2.5.5. Optimised Vessel Design At UAE Ports

The next theme of the literature review is optimising vessel design and operations in seaports is imperative to enhance economic and environmental performance. The research by An and colleagues (2021) is on closed-loop shipping systems in the Middle East's hydrocarbon industry. The research has employed a detailed simulation model to assess economic and environmental performance through consideration of uncertainties like weather and port operations. The research has integrated an optimisation model into the simulation to prescribe the optimal number of vessels and voyage speed based on the requirement of ports that introduced a novel large-vessel-first-use dispatching policy. The research results have revealed significant potential for cost savings of 26.8% and a reduction of greenhouse gas emissions by 39% compared to current operations that emphasised the benefits of utilizing large vessels and adopting slower voyage speeds. Another article by Buonomano and colleagues (2023) explored the growing energy demand in harbour areas that emphasised the need to reduce pollutant emissions. The research has presented a dynamic simulation model to assess and optimise the energy and economic impact of ports. This includes the integration of renewable energy sources, alternative fuels, and thermal energy networks through a multi-objective optimisation approach through consideration of energy and economic indexes. The case study of the port of Naples demonstrates the model's capability has showcased the potential for high rates of renewable energy production on-site i.e., 84% along with significant contributions to decarbonization and pollutant emission reduction. Another article by Abou Kasm and colleagues (2021) has addressed vessel scheduling complexities at seaports through consideration of pilotage and tugging constraints in berthing operations. A mixed-integer programming formulation and an exact solution approach are proposed that showed significant improvements, especially during congestion periods when compared to the traditional first-come first-serve policy. Hence, the study introduced a novel approach that simultaneously considers pilotage and tugging requirements to enhance the efficiency of vessel scheduling in real-size cases. Moreover, findings by Nguyen Minh and colleagues (2021) have provided a novel framework for port investment optimisation is presented that is composed of a three-stage process. The approach included a performance-based analysis to determine operational safety policies, a discrete event simulation model to assess port performance under various investment scenarios, and an optimisation model to generate optimal investment planning. Thus, the case study of Lien Chieu Port demonstrated the effectiveness of the framework to balance port dimensions and cargo handling rates that offer a practical and comprehensive method to optimise port investments. Finally, the article by Yuan and colleagues (2023) have addressed IMO's carbon intensity indicator (CII) regulation to reduce carbon emissions in the shipping industry. The study has proposed an operational efficiency optimisation approach for short-term upgrades of existing fleets to meet CII requirements. The model has estimated the annual attained CII of a ship considering different speed and route choices that optimised vessel schedules to maximise annual fleet profit along with compliance of CII ratings. Hence, the research results implied that specific routes can offer inherent advantages in emission reduction, and the proposed method proves versatile to support fleet operational decisions for meeting decarbonization regulations. All these research articles regarding optimised vessel design and operations at seaports underscore the importance of advanced simulation models, multi-objective optimisation, and innovative approaches to address various complexities in shipping systems. Therefore, these studies collectively contribute valuable insights to improve economic efficiency and reduce environmental impacts that pave the way for sustainable practices in maritime operations.

2.5.6. Case Studies of UAE Ports

The pieces of research on UAE ports are reflected in the selected case studies that include diverse aspects ranging from sustainable development goals and international cooperation to green building regulations, Six Sigma deployment, and the transformative potential of blockchain in supply chain activities. An article by Krzymowski (2020) has delved into the UAE's ambitious initiatives that emphasise the analysis of SDGs in the Arab region that is focused on the UAE's exemplary projects. The research has covered Vision 2021, the Green

Economy Program, the National Innovation Strategy, and the Energy 2050 Strategy along with others. This piece of research has highlighted the socio-political dimensions of sustainable development, the impact of technology, and the significance of events like the World Expo in Dubai. Hence, the article has positioned the UAE's dynamic population growth against the backdrop of its impressive socio-economic and technological advancements. Another article by Krzymowski (2022) has explored the Three Seas Initiative (3SI) and its impact on the relationship between the UAE and Central and Eastern European countries. The findings have investigated the extent to which high-level visits facilitate trade exchanges and explore prospects for cooperation in energy transformation and green economy initiatives. In this regard, the research has employed quantitative methods and case studies that revealed that regular top-level visits indeed support trade and unveil strategic potential for energy transformation that emphasises the growing ties between the UAE and 3SI countries. Another article by Najini and colleagues (2020) is focused on green building regulations in the UAE, particularly in emirates like Abu Dhabi, Dubai, and Sharjah. The research has addressed the gap in existing literature through a techno-economic cross-code analysis of various green building regulations. Thus, the research by the use of a case study of an existing high-rise green office building has evaluated energy and water performance that provides a comprehensive economic study based on the discounted cash flow technique. These findings have offered valuable insights into cost-effective trade-offs that aid decision-makers in choosing appropriate green building regulations. Moreover, an article by Bhat and colleagues (2023) has explicated the deployment and sustainment of Six Sigma for service quality improvement in the UAE. The research has employed an exploratory research methodology with multiple case studies regarding the motivation, key factors, tools, challenges, and performance impact of implementing Six Sigma in four different organisations. The research underscored the significance of internal customer feedback, KPIs, and CTQs in Six Sigma projects that accentuate the role of top management leadership and effective communication. Lastly, the article by L. Li and Zhou (2021) has discussed the transformative potential of blockchain in supply chain activities, specifically within the maritime and shipping industry. The article has summarized research articles from 2015 to 2018 that outlined key enabling technologies and blockchain structures, and presented seven case studies that illustrate the impact of blockchain on supply chain management objectives. The research findings have provided early evidence linking blockchain deployment to increased transparency and accountability that portrays the potential to revolutionize key aspects of supply chain management. Hence, the literature review of UAE ports is evidenced by these case studies that revealed a multifaceted landscape that is composed of sustainable development, international cooperation, green regulations, process improvement methodologies, and cutting-edge technologies such as blockchain.

2.6. Research Gap

The literature review has presented a comprehensive overview of sustainable practices within the UAE maritime industry that is grounded in three key theoretical perspectives i.e., innovation diffusion theory, sustainable development theory, and environmental policy theory. The conceptual framework has integrated these theories to understand the adoption of environmentally friendly practices and technology in UAE ports. The study is focused on critical aspects that include sustainable shipping management, clean energy technologies, and maritime shipping digitization. Though the literature has offered valuable insights, a noticeable research gap exists in the context of a holistic and integrated understanding of how these sustainable practices interact and contribute to the comprehensive goals of environmental sustainability, economic efficiency, and regulatory compliance in the UAE maritime sector.

Firstly, the theme of "Environment-Friendly Practices at UAE Ports" has explored various aspects like market entry strategies for sustainable products, challenges and opportunities in digital transformation, and the impact of green maritime transportation on emissions reduction. However, the literature review has lacked a synthesized analysis that connects these diverse elements to provide a unified understanding of how digital transformation, sustainable facility management, and supply chain sustainability collectively contribute to the overarching goal of environmental sustainability in UAE ports. The research question aims to address this gap through the investigation of how these individual aspects intersect and contribute to the holistic adoption of environmentally friendly practices depending on the challenges and opportunities presented in the dynamic landscape of UAE ports. Similarly, in the exploration of "Solar Power at UAE Ports," the literature review has discussed the utilization of solar energy, hydrogen production, and the feasibility of renewable energy sources in UAE ports. Though individual studies shed light on specific aspects, there is a gap in connecting these findings to creating a cohesive narrative on the integration of solar power in UAE ports. Therefore, the research question aims to address this gap through an investigation of how various solar energy initiatives like hydrogen production and on-site renewable energy projects can be strategically integrated to optimise energy usage and contribute to the broader sustainability goals of UAE ports. Moreover, the section on "Wind Energy at UAE Ports" has provided insights into the feasibility and challenges of wind energy adoption that include offshore wind projects and the integration of marine renewable sources. However, there is a need for a more comprehensive understanding of how wind energy solutions like offshore wind farms and tidal energy can be strategically combined with logistics solutions to enhance the overall sustainability of UAE ports. So, the research question intends to explore how wind energy projects can be optimised in conjunction with logistical innovations to address economic and environmental considerations simultaneously. Furthermore, the examination of "Innovative Propulsion Systems at UAE Ports" has discussed the transition to electric propulsion, renewable fuels, and disruptive innovations in the maritime sector. Despite individual insights into each aspect, there is a research gap to understand how these propulsion systems can be strategically chosen and integrated to optimise both economic and environmental performance in UAE ports. The research question helps to address this gap through the investigation of the criteria to select and optimise innovative propulsion systems for meeting the dual objectives of efficiency and sustainability in the maritime industry. Lastly, the theme of "Optimised Vessel Design at UAE Ports" has explored closed-loop shipping systems, vessel scheduling complexities, and port investment optimisation. However, a research gap exists to synthesize these findings to provide a comprehensive analysis of how optimised vessel design, efficient scheduling, and strategic port investments collectively contribute to the overarching goals of economic and environmental performance in UAE ports. Hence, the research question aims to address this gap through an examination of how these elements can be strategically aligned to achieve a sustainable and efficient maritime operation. In summary, the literature review has provided valuable insights into various facets of sustainable practices within UAE ports, but a research gap exists to synthesize these findings to develop a holistic understanding of the integrated strategies needed to achieve sustainability goals.

2.7. Summary and Transition

This chapter stands out as the most comprehensive, delving into the historical and theoretical facets of the research topic. The literature review is conducted meticulously, offering in-depth insights into various key areas such as maritime energy management, green practices, sustainability, solar power, wind energy, innovative propulsion systems, and optimised vessel design. Having established the foundation and identified gaps in the literature, the next chapter will shift focus toward devising a methodology. This methodology aims to provide a primary stance on the research topic by employing data collection methods and surveys.

Chapter 3

Research Method

The literature review has provided a comprehensive exploration of sustainable practices in the UAE maritime industry that has explicated environment-friendly practices, solar power utilization, wind energy adoption, innovative propulsion systems, and optimised vessel design. Though individual studies have contributed valuable insights, the literature review has revealed a research gap in synthesizing these aspects into a holistic understanding of how diverse sustainable practices interact and collectively contribute to the comprehensive efficiency and health of the marine environment in UAE ports. Keeping the viewpoints of the literature review and research question intact, it is necessary to make a few changes to the hypothesis. This restated research question helps to target the literature gap.

RQ: To what extent are environment-friendly practices embraced by UAE ports and shipping companies in the short term, and what is the collective impact of these initiatives on the efficiency and health of the marine environment?

H00: There is no substantial embracement of environment-friendly practices in the short term at UAE ports and shipping companies. Moreover, there is no significant impact of these initiatives on the efficiency and health of the marine environment.

H01: There is a practical embracement of environment-friendly practices in the short term by UAE ports and shipping companies. Furthermore, there is a positive and significant impact of these initiatives on the efficiency and health of the marine environment.

The restated version of the question and hypothesis has directly addressed the identified research gap from the research review. The revised question has emphasised the need to investigate the collective and integrated impact of various sustainable practices on UAE ports that are aligned with the interconnected nature of these practices discussed in the literature. The hypothesis has suggested a shift from a null assumption of no embracement or impact to an affirmative stance that acknowledges practical embracement and a significantly positive impact on marine efficiency and health. Hence, the rephrased question aims to guide the primary research to explore the synergies among different sustainable initiatives and their overall influence on the UAE maritime industry.

3.1. Research Design and Rationale

The research design for the primary quantitative research includes the use of surveys to collect data on the embracement of environment-friendly practices (Bloomfield & Fisher, 2019). These practices include solar power, wind energy, innovative propulsion systems, and optimised vessel design by UAE ports and shipping companies. The data collected from the surveys is subjected to statistical analyses through t-tests and ANOVA variance tests to evaluate the validity of the formulated hypotheses (Mishra et al., 2019). The choice of a survey as the primary data collection method is grounded in its ability to efficiently collect large-scale quantitative data from diverse respondents. Surveys are a standardized approach that ensures consistency in data collection and enables the collection of a wide range of responses across various dimensions of sustainable practices (Ball, 2019). The structured nature of surveys assists the quantitative measurement of embracement levels that allows for statistical analyses to test the formulated hypotheses rigorously. The selection of the t-test as a statistical tool is to compare the means of two groups, which for this research is the embracement levels of environment-friendly practices by UAE ports and shipping companies. Thus, through the application of the t-test, the research can assess whether there is a significant difference between the observed and expected means that provides statistical evidence for or against the null hypothesis that there is no substantial embracement. Additionally, the use of ANOVA variance tests is justified to extend the analysis beyond a binary comparison since it allows for the examination of embracement levels across multiple groups, like different types of environment-friendly practices or various ports and shipping companies. This method adds granularity to the analysis that captures the potential variations among different sustainable initiatives along with their impact on the marine environment. The feasibility of the chosen research design is supported by various factors. Firstly, surveys are cost-effective and efficient in terms of data collection, especially when a diverse group of respondents is targeted like maritime industry professionals, port authorities, and shipping company representatives. The structured format of surveys ensures clarity and consistency in responses and reduces the likelihood of ambiguity or misinterpretation. Furthermore, the use of quantitative methods like t-tests and ANOVA adds a robust statistical foundation to the research since these tests provide objective and measurable outcomes that allow for a clear assessment of the hypotheses. The quantitative nature of the data also facilitates the application of statistical software for analysis that enhances the precision and reliability of results. However, it is essential to acknowledge potential challenges in survey-based research like the possibility of response bias or limited generalizability. Thus, efforts should be made to ensure a representative sample to reach out to a diverse range of stakeholders within the UAE maritime industry. Additionally, survey questions must be carefully designed to capture nuanced aspects of sustainable practices and their impact on the marine environment. Hence, the proposed research design has employed surveys and statistical tests that offer a systematic and feasible approach to investigate the embracement of environment-friendly practices in UAE ports and shipping companies.

3.2. Methodology

Aprimary research questionnaire was developed that could be shared with the research sample. The questionnaire for the participants of the research is shown in Appendix B. This questionnaire was the next step of the primary research where the initial step was the consent from the participants. The research aimed to target 30 professionals from the ports of UAE and to gather their consent, the forms were signed. The people who had signed the forms were from the maritime industry and they belonged to UAE ports and shipping companies. To conduct the primary research, there was an incessant need to get consent as it ensured confidentiality and maintenance of personal information throughout the research. The research consent is shown in Appendix A; the form was shared with all the candidates of the survey.

3.2.1. Population

The first step of the research is to select the population from an accurate method. The population selected for this research consists of professionals who are working at UAE ports and shipping companies. These workers include port managers, shipping company managers, and employees involved in various capacities within the maritime industry. Given the scale and nature of the research, a sample size of 30 participants has been chosen for the survey, which is a reasonable one to test for the hypothesis. This sample size allowed for a focused investigation along with the maintenance of a manageable and feasible approach. The survey aims to capture diverse perspectives within the industry to ensure a representative snapshot of embracement levels of environment-friendly practices. The confidence interval chosen for this research is set at 95% where this confidence level indicates that the survey was conducted numerous times. This implies that the true population parameter falls within the calculated interval for 95% of those surveys which adds robustness and reliability to the findings. Note that for this research, sample size is appropriate, which has a margin of error of ±5%. This selection helps to keep the calculations simple while properly sampling the participants through convenience sampling a form of random sampling that helps in bias-free collection of data.

3.2.2. Sampling and Sampling Procedures

This research aimed to know the extent of environment-friendly practices, including solar power, wind energy, innovative propulsion systems, and optimised vessel design that were embraced by UAE ports and shipping companies along with the collective impact of these practices. The sampling method to choose the participants for this research was convenience sampling which was suitable for practical considerations of a targeted population i.e., UAE in this case. It is a non-probability technique that the researchers use to select the participants depending on the ease and need for sorting the sample. This was the most feasible approach that represented the participants in the most unbiased manner (Bhardwaj, 2019). The ports in UAE are always in a state of hustle and rush since they are the busiest ports in terms of trade and tourism. Therefore, to ensure accurate information, stratification is not a suitable option since it can affect the transparency of the research. Furthermore, the use of convenience sampling was suggested because it is cost-effective, accessible, and meets the practical constraints of shipping and maritime energy management. However, this mode of sampling can induce sampling bias, but it does not affect the scope of the research as the identity of participants is kept confidential and anonymous. Thus, through this sampling, insights were gathered to understand the general trends at UAE ports. This research through a stepwise assessment of survey findings that aimed to draw relations between different aspects of the shipping industry and companies that met sustainability through green initiatives. The research employed statistical techniques that can derive appropriate results that have significant importance in terms of the research question and its hypothesis. The research questionnaire is divided into sections and the first section helps in sampling the data; using the findings from section 1, the following table is presented. Moreover, each of the survey findings in quantitative form is presented in the form of tables.

Table 3.

Participants Responses for Section 1

	Section 1		
Participant No	Section 1.1 (role)	Section 1.2 (years)	Section 1.3 (port)
1	Port manager	10	Port Khalifa, Abu Dhabi
2	Port manager	2	Mina Zayed, Abu Dhabi
3	Port manager	4	Musaffah Port, Abu Dhabi

4	Port manager	5	Port Jebel Ali, Dubai
5	Port manager	6	Mina Rashid, Dubai
6	Port manager	7	Mina Al Hamriyah, Dubai
7	Shipping company manager	2	Port Khalifa, Abu Dhabi
8	Shipping company manager	1	Mina Zayed, Abu Dhabi
9	Shipping company manager	4	Musaffah Port, Abu Dhabi
10	Shipping company manager	6	Port Jebel Ali, Dubai
11	Shipping company manager	7	Mina Rashid, Dubai
12	Shipping company manager	8	Mina Al Hamriyah, Dubai
13	Port employee	8	Port Khalifa, Abu Dhabi
14	Port employee	9	Mina Zayed, Abu Dhabi
15	Port employee	6	Musaffah Port, Abu Dhabi
16	Port employee	1	Port Jebel Ali, Dubai
17	Port employee	11	Mina Rashid, Dubai
18	Port employee	3	Mina Al Hamriyah, Dubai
19	Shipping company employee	1	Port Khalifa, Abu Dhabi
20	Shipping company employee	7	Mina Zayed, Abu Dhabi
21	Shipping company employee	1.5	Musaffah Port, Abu Dhabi
22	Shipping company employee	9	Port Jebel Ali, Dubai
23	Shipping company employee	10	Mina Rashid, Dubai
24	Shipping company employee	1	Mina Al Hamriyah, Dubai
25	Port employee	12	Port Khalifa, Abu Dhabi
26	Port employee	9	Mina Zayed, Abu Dhabi
27	Port employee	8	Musaffah Port, Abu Dhabi
28	Shipping company employee	2	Port Jebel Ali, Dubai
29	Shipping company employee	5	Mina Rashid, Dubai
30	Shipping company employee	7	Mina Al Hamriyah, Dubai

This is the basic sample and the demographic data of the participants is gathered from section 1. This data helps in the descriptive analysis of the parameters that help to develop subjective opinions on the research participants and further findings.

Table 4.

Data collected from the survey

Participant No	Section 1.4 (Gender)	Section 1.5 (Age)
1	Male	42
2	Male	38
3	Female	32
4	Male	31
5	Female	25
6	Male	25
7	Male	20
8	Male	28
9	Female	23
10	Male	26

11	Male	37
12	Male	28
13	Male	38
14	Male	29
15	Male	26
16	Male	23
17	Male	25
18	Male	31
19	Male	33
20	Male	43
21	Male	32
22	Male	29
23	Male	24
24	Male	34
25	Male	31
26	Male	44
27	Male	26
28	Female	37
29	Male	35
30	Female	38

This was the basic data of the study that described the statistical data in the data analysis. It also helped to devise characteristics of the data sample in the form of descriptive statistics.

3.2.3. Procedures for Recruitment, Participation, and Data Collection (Primary Data)

The research process is systematically designed in a series of steps, facilitating the effective investigation of the research question and enabling the testing of hypotheses. The first step is to ensure that the findings of the research are primary and are not colluded in any form. All the participants from the UAE ports are willing to be a part of the survey. For this purpose, a detailed consent form is made and signed by all the 30 participants. See Appendix A for the consent form that states the scope, purpose, and aim of the research. This helped to ensure that the participants were not forced. Since the data is collected based on convenience sampling, it is ensured that all the participants belong to UAE ports and know about the implementation of green initiatives. This aspect ensures that all the participants are selected on merit and they provide accurate information based on their observations at the respective ports of Abu Dhabi and Dubai. The questionnaire prepared for the participants is annexed in Appendix B. This helps to know about the use of solar energy, wind power, innovative propulsion systems, and optimised vessel design at UAE ports. The questions of the survey are designed in a way that the research variables are assessed by the use of statistical tests i.e., t-test and ANOVA variance test. To ensure the reliability of responses, the questionnaire for the survey was focused on clarity and comprehensibility. The survey was then electronically administered to participants to facilitate their engagement, and responses were collected within the stipulated timeframe (Ball, 2019). Subsequently, the collected data underwent a meticulous process that started with entry and organisation in a spreadsheet. This step was important to check the accuracy of the data and identify any potential errors during sorting. The organised data was then imported into statistical software i.e., SPSS, for the final phase of analysis (Okagbue et al., 2021). Initially, descriptive statistics were also employed to provide a concise summary and visual representation of key findings that offer an overview of central tendencies and variations related to the embracement of environment-friendly practices in UAE ports and shipping companies. To address the research question and hypotheses, t-tests were applied to assess significant differences in the impact of green practices on the environment at UAE ports. The analysis sought to test the formulated null hypothesis (H00) against the alternative hypothesis (H01) where ANOVA variance tests were utilized to explore potential differences across various groups that investigate how variations in green practices impact the adoption of green practices for maritime energy management among different sectors within UAE ports. This systematic research process ensured a comprehensive journey from participant consent and survey administration to robust data collection and advanced statistical analysis that are aligned with the objectives of the current research on the embracement of environment-friendly practices and their impact on marine efficiency in the UAE maritime industry.

3.2.4. Intervention

The intervention in this research involves an investigation of the embracement of environment-friendly practices in UAE ports and shipping companies that are focused on solar power utilization, wind energy adoption, innovative propulsion systems, and optimised vessel design. The independent variables for the t-test and ANOVA variance test include the sustainable practices under consideration along with their respective levels of embracement by the ports and shipping companies. The dependent variable is the cumulative impact of these practices on the efficiency and health of the marine environment. Now to apply the intervention, the first step is to conduct a t-test where the independent variable of embracement levels of environment-friendly practices by UAE ports and shipping companies, and the dependent variable of the overall impact on the marine environment's efficiency and health are utilized. This test aimed to compare the means of two groups to assess whether there is a significant difference between observed and expected means. It also validifies the hypothesis such that the null hypothesis (H00) suggests no substantial embracement or impact, while the alternative hypothesis (H01) posits practical embracement and a significant impact on marine efficiency and health. Then the ANOVA variance test is applied to independent variables i.e., different types of environment-friendly practices that include solar power, wind energy, innovative propulsion systems, and optimised vessel design at various ports and shipping companies. The dependent variable remains the collective impact of these practices on the marine environment. This statistical tool allows for the examination of embracement levels across multiple groups that provides a more comprehensive analysis of potential variations among different sustainable initiatives and their impact on the marine environment. Hence, the t-test and ANOVA variance test are employed as key interventions to analyse the relationship between the embracement of environment-friendly practices and their impact on the efficiency and health of the marine environment through a consideration of different variables and groups within the UAE maritime industry. Finally, qualitative analysis is also executed to get an insight into participants' perspectives on the use of the maritime industry by using the questionnaire.

3.2.5. Instrumentation and Operationalization of Constructs

The success of any quantitative research relies heavily on the precision of measurement instruments and the accurate operationalization of constructs. In this research, the focus is to evaluate the embracement of environment-friendly practices at UAE ports and shipping companies where the instruments used are primarily the survey questionnaire and statistical tools for analysis. These instruments are carefully designed to ensure the reliable measurement of variables and the testing of hypotheses i.e., a survey is prepared in coherence with the basic findings and background of the topic. The survey questionnaire, in this case, served as the primary instrument for data collection that aimed to capture the embracement levels of various environment-friendly practices and their collective impact on the efficiency and health of the marine environment. Hence, to ensure the accuracy and effectiveness of this instrument, every construct is operationalized with meticulous attention to detail. Firstly, the constructs associated with environment-friendly practices include solar power utilization, wind energy adoption, innovative propulsion systems, and optimised vessel design. These constructs are operationalized through specific survey questions tailored to each practice where respondents are asked to indicate the extent to which their respective ports or shipping companies embrace solar power through a range from minimal to extensive embracement. Similar questions are structured for wind energy, innovative propulsion systems, and optimised vessel design to ensure a comprehensive evaluation of the embracement levels of each practice. Secondly, the construct related to the collective impact of these practices on the marine environment is operationalized by the use of survey questions that assess the perceived efficiency and health outcomes. In this case, the respondents are prompted to provide their opinions on the observed improvements or lack in marine efficiency and health due to the implemented sustainable practices. Moreover, a Likert scale is employed for quantifying these qualitative responses that range from no observed impact to a significant positive impact. Moving to the statistical tools, the t-test is instrumental in assessing the means of two groups which are the embracement levels of environment-friendly practices and the impact on the marine environment. The independent variable for the t-test corresponds to the measured levels of embracement, operationalized through survey responses. Meanwhile, the dependent variable is the observed impact on marine efficiency and health. Similarly, the ANOVA variance test has extended the analysis to multiple groups that examine potential variations among different types of environment-friendly practices and various ports and shipping companies. The independent variables for the ANOVA are the different categories within these sustainable initiatives, operationalized through the respective survey questions although the dependent variable remains the collective impact on the marine environment. Thus, the instrumentation and operationalization of constructs for this research are paramount to ensure the accuracy and reliability of data collection and analysis. It is because the survey questionnaire is strategically designed to quantitatively measure embracement levels and their impact by the use of statistical tools such as the t-test and ANOVA provide a robust framework for hypothesis testing across various constructs within the UAE maritime industry. Therefore, the impact of each variable is observed through the t-test and ANOVA variance test in the context of these instruments and operationalized constructs.

3.2.6. Intervention Applications That Involve Manipulation of an Independent Variable

In the realm of research, intervention applications entail the deliberate manipulation of an independent variable, a pivotal element in experimental designs. This manipulation enables researchers to exercise control over specific factors, facilitating the observation of their impact on the dependent variable. These interventions are particularly valuable to establish causal relationships and inform evidence-based practices. The manipulation of an independent variable involves intentional change or a control factor to observe its impact on the outcome i.e., the dependent variable. In the context of the current research focused on environment-friendly practices in UAE ports and shipping companies, an intervention application includes the deliberate implementation of sustainable initiatives like the introduction of solar power systems, wind energy utilization, innovative propulsion systems, or optimised vessel designs. Hence, the researchers can observe and measure its effects on the dependent variable (efficiency and health of marine environment) through manipulation of the independent variable, which in this case is the degree of embracement of these sustainable practices. In this regard, a controlled intervention is considered in one port where a comprehensive embracement of solar power technology is implemented, while another port maintains its conventional energy practices. The embracement level becomes the manipulated independent variable, and its impact on the efficiency and health of the marine environment acts as the dependent variable. Hence, through systematic data collection and analysis, researchers can assess whether the manipulated variable of embracement of solar power has a significant effect on the observed outcomes or not. These intervention applications involve the manipulation of an independent variable that offers a controlled environment to draw causal inferences and contribute to the development of evidence-based policies. In the context of sustainable practices, such interventions could inform decision-makers about the effectiveness of specific initiatives that guide the industry toward environmentally friendly alternatives. However, it is important to note that ethical considerations must be paramount in the implementation of green initiatives to ensure that the manipulation does not cause harm and that the benefits outweigh any potential risks. Therefore, intervention applications involving the manipulation of an independent variable are powerful tools in research, allowing for controlled experiments that can establish causal relationships. In the context of environment-friendly practices in UAE ports and shipping companies, these interventions provide a means to systematically study the impact of sustainable initiatives on the efficiency and health of the marine environment that offer valuable insights for both academia and industry stakeholders.

3.3. Data Analysis Plan

Data analysis planning is an important part of research as it guides the steps to be implemented for conducting a quantitative statistical analysis by the use of t-tests and ANOVA variance test. This plan envisages a stepwise procedure to be implemented for data collection and analysis. The purpose of this research is to know about the endorsement of green practices at UAE ports and its impact on efficiency. For this purpose, the t-test and ANOVA variance test is used. To implement these tests, the first step is to collect the data by organising it in the form of tables and avoiding any values that lie outside the range or are inconsistent. In the dataset, each variable is distinctly presented to show the responses of participants along with their personal perspectives. The next step of analysis is to conduct descriptive analysis through the calculation of measures of central tendency where graphs and tables of the data are presented. Once descriptive analysis is performed, the t-test is applied to compare the means of two groups i.e., independent and dependent variables to test the hypothesis through the value of p. Note that if the value of p is less than the significance level of 0.05, then the alternate hypothesis is true and vice versa. Once the t-test is conducted, the ANOVA variance test is applied to compare the multiple groups and to test the hypothesis. The findings from the tests are practical and have specific implications for the existing sustainable practices at UAE ports. Hence, this is the data analysis plan that is to be followed for the given sample size where each of the data constraints is properly labelled and presented for analysis about the embracement of green practices at UAE ports and shipping companies.

3.4. Threats to Validity

External validity, internal validity, and construct validity are three types of threats to quantitative research. Each of these threats is discussed in detail from the research implementation perspective. Moreover, this section also discusses the ethical considerations necessary for the research that helps to know about the concerns that need to be mitigated.

3.4.1. External Validity

External validity threats refer to potential limitations in the generalizability of findings of the research to broader populations or settings. In the context of the current research on the embracement of environment-friendly practices in UAE ports and shipping companies, a few external validity threats should be considered. Firstly, population validity is a concern since the research relies on a sample of 30 professionals from UAE ports and shipping companies, which is not a full representation of the entire population in this industry. The sample size and the specific demographic characteristics of the participants like their roles, years of experience, and ports of operation can limit the generalizability of the findings to a wider range of maritime professionals. The research can be more robust if it included a more diverse and extensive sample that captures a broader spectrum of perspectives within the UAE maritime industry such that this approach can be opted for by future researchers. The second threat of external validity is associated with ecology which pertains to the extent to which the study conditions and settings mimic real-world situations. Another threat is temporal validity where the research captures a snapshot of the current state of environment-friendly practices in UAE ports, but these practices are subject to change over time due to technological advancements, policy shifts, or industry trends. The findings will not hold true in the future, as the maritime industry evolves where longitudinal studies or periodic assessments are more beneficial to track changes and ensure the relevance and applicability of the research findings over time. Additionally, cultural and contextual factors pose a threat to external validity where the embracement of sustainable practices can be influenced by cultural attitudes, regional policies, and economic considerations. The findings of this research cannot be easily transferable to maritime industries in other regions with different socio-economic and cultural contexts. A comparative analysis with other regions or consideration of these contextual factors in the interpretation of findings can be efficiently used to enhance the external validity of the research. Hence, this research design provided valuable insights into the embracement of environment-friendly practices in UAE ports and shipping companies where external validity threats must be acknowledged to address the threats and strengthen the research findings by accurate research development.

3.4.2. Internal Validity

Threats to internal validity encompass potential obstacles that can impact the precision and dependability of causal inferences in a research study. In the context of the ongoing research, the focus is environmentally friendly practices in UAE ports and shipping companies where it is essential to address several internal validity concerns. One of the significant threats is selection bias since the research employs convenience sampling to select participants, which can introduce bias if certain groups within the population are systematically excluded. For example, the findings can be skewed because professionals who are more environmentally conscious or involved in sustainable initiatives are more likely to participate. To mitigate this threat, the researchers can employ more rigorous sampling techniques or consider the use of stratified sampling to ensure a more representative selection of participants, but it is avoided in this case to keep the general ideas from all the ports intact. The second potential internal validity threat is the possibility of social desirability bias in survey responses since the participants can be inclined to provide answers that they perceive as socially acceptable or align with the perceived expectations of environmentally friendly practices. This bias could increase the reported levels of embracement of sustainable practices where the technique of anonymous survey is used to provide responses and enhance the reliability of the findings. Furthermore, there is a risk of measurement error, especially in self-reported survey data as participants have varying interpretations of terminologies like "environment-friendly practices" which leads to inconsistencies in their responses. To address this, it is ensured that survey questions are clear, unambiguous, and aligned with the definitions established in the literature. Lastly, the research design is of a cross-sectional nature that poses a threat to internal validity as the study captures a snapshot of embracement levels at a specific point in time, making it challenging to establish causation. In this regard, longitudinal studies tracking changes in sustainable practices over time can strengthen the internal validity of causal claims that provide a more nuanced understanding of the dynamics within the UAE maritime industry. Thus, though the research design is robust internal validity threats related to selection bias, social desirability bias, measurement error, and the cross-sectional nature of the study should be carefully considered to provide concrete findings.

3.4.3. Construct Validity

Construct validity threats in the current research on environment-friendly practices in UAE ports and shipping companies contain concerns related to the accurate measurement and operationalization of key constructs. One potential threat is the issue of content validity in the survey instrument that occurs if the selected survey questions fail to comprehensively capture the various dimensions of environment-friendly practices that compromise the construct validity of the research. To mitigate this threat, it is ensured that the survey items are aligned with the definitions and components identified in the literature review. There is also a need to conduct a thorough content validity assessment through expert reviews that can enhance the alignment between the survey questions and the intended constructs to ensure that accurate information is provided. Additionally, there is a risk of mono-operation bias, where a single method i.e., the survey is utilized to measure complex constructs such as embracement of environment-friendly practices. Another risk of construct validity is the over-generalizability of the multifaceted nature of sustainability initiatives in the maritime industry. To address this, future researchers can employ a multimethod approach that combines survey data with other sources such as interviews, observations, or archival records. Lastly, the risk of construct underrepresentation must be considered that occurs if the survey fails to include all relevant facets of environment-friendly practices. So, continuous refinement of survey items based on ongoing literature reviews and industry insights is important to address this threat and ensure the construct validity of the research. Therefore, it is important to address construct validity threats in the research involves careful consideration of content validity, potential biases, and the need for a comprehensive measurement approach through employing diverse data collection methods and refining survey instruments

3.4.4. Ethical Procedures

In this research, ethical procedures were ensured throughout the research, these measures help to maintain the well-being of the participants of the research. The ethical considerations for this research include informed consent from all the participants while maintaining confidentiality of the findings through anonymity while conducting the survey. These steps are performed during the recruitment process where all the participants showed their consent and responded voluntarily. In this case, convenience sampling is also a manifestation that all participants willingly became a part of the research and they honestly shared their opinions about green practices at UAE ports. This data is also kept in secure form and all the data is stored in the form of tables following the ethical guidelines. Hence, the research maintained all rules of ethicality, integrity, respect, autonomy, and confidentiality of conducting research.

3.5. Summary

This chapter extensively details the methodology employed, incorporating the use of the t-test and ANOVA variance test. The stepwise presentation of actions within this chapter serves to clarify the research's validity. The methodology outlined here forms the basis for data analysis, which is further explored in the upcoming chapter. The subsequent chapter will delve into the collected data and present the results.

Chapter 4

RESULTS

This chapter presents the results in graphical and tabulated forms, offering a visual and numerical elucidation of the findings. The data is analysed through both statistical results and descriptive analysis, providing an in-depth investigation of the research question from a statistical perspective. The data collection process is structured to facilitate the appropriate application of ANOVA variance and t-test methodologies.

4.1. Data Collection

The survey is performed and the data is collected, which is presented here. The data from sections 2 and 3 is about the quantitative scenario regarding the embracement of green shipping practices. Firstly, the data collection of the t-test is done which is shown below.

Table 5.

Collected Data for T-test

Participant No.	Independent Variable Section 2				Dependent Variables Section 3	
	2.1	2.2	2.3	2.4	3.1	3.2
1	0	1	1	3	2	3
2	2	2	1	3	3	3
3	1	1	1	3	4	3
4	0	3	0	3	3	3
5	1	4	0	4	3	3
6	2	3	0	4	3	4
7	0	3	0	4	3	4
8	0	3	0	4	3	4
9	0	2	0	4	2	4
10	2	2	0	4	2	4
11	1	2	0	4	2	4
12	2	3	1	4	2	3
13	1	3	1	2	3	3
14	1	3	2	3	3	4
15	1	3	2	4	3	4
16	1	3	1	3	3	3
17	0	2	1	2	4	4
18	1	2	1	4	3	4
19	0	2	1	4	3	3
20	1	2	1	4	3	3
21	0	1	0	2	4	4
22	1	1	0	3	3	4

23	0	1	0	4	3	3
24	0	1	0	3	4	4
25	0	1	0	4	3	3
26	1	3	0	3	4	4
27	2	2	0	3	3	3
28	1	2	0	3	3	3
29	1	2	0	4	4	4
30	0	3	0	4	4	3

Now, to apply the ANOVA variance test, it is important to observe the efficiency of green practices and their impact on the sustainability of the maritime industry on a scale of 0 to 5.

Table 6.

Collected Data for ANOVA test

Participant No.	Section 3	
	Group 1 (3.1)	Group 2 (3.2)
1	2	3
2	3	3
3	4	3
4	3	3
5	3	3
6	3	4
7	3	4
8	3	4
9	2	4
10	2	4
11	2	4
12	2	3
13	3	3
14	3	4
15	3	4
16	3	3
17	4	4
18	3	4
19	3	3
20	3	3
21	4	4
22	3	4
23	3	3
24	4	4
25	3	3
26	4	4
27	3	3
28	3	3
29	4	4
30	4	3

Though the study is quantitative, there is a need to know about the qualitative ideas of the research topic. To gather qualitative information section 4 is prepared as an optional part that is filled by a few research participants. One participant emphasised the endorsement of solar energy at each port in the UAE. Another participant highlighted the sustainability of wind energy that underscores its role in maintaining a green environment, especially when coupled with innovative vessel design. Lastly, a participant inferred that innovative propulsion systems stand out as a solution that provides both efficiency and environmental sustainability within the UAE's maritime energy sector.

4.2. Treatment and/or Intervention Fidelity

This research has adopted a multifaceted approach to present the findings. Firstly, descriptive statistics are employed, accompanied by bar charts that offer a comprehensive overview of the quantitative data collected on the embracement of green shipping practices in section 2 of the questionnaire and their impact on efficiency and marine environment sustainability in section 3. This graphical representation through bar charts provides visually discerning patterns and trends within the data. Subsequently, the t-test findings are presented that are supported by a p-plot to rigorously analyse the statistical significance of differences between groups in terms of embracing environment-friendly practices. Hence, this layered approach ensures a nuanced understanding of the research question that blends both quantitative and qualitative insights for a comprehensive evaluation of UAE ports and shipping companies' sustainability initiatives.

4.3. Study Results
4.3.1. Statistical Analysis
To know about the sample data used and the participants of the research, descriptive analysis is conducted on SPSS. The following are the findings of measures of central tendency of the descriptive aspects of the participants based on demography.

Table 7.

Descriptive Analysis of the Participants

Statistics

		Role	Experience	Port_Name	Gender	Age
N	Valid	30	30	30	30	30
	Missing	0	9	0	0	9
Mean			5.7500			31.1000
Median			6.0000			31.0000
Mode			1.00[a]			25.00[a]
Std. Deviation			3.32895			6.40770
Variance			11.082			41.059
Range			11.00			24.00
Sum			172.50			933.00

a. Multiple modes exist. The smallest value is shown

The descriptive data is also shown in the form of bar charts below (with percentages).
For descriptive analysis, it is essential to assess frequency tables on SPSS where the table has shown that 23.1% of participants are port employees, 15.4% are port managers, 23.1% are shipping company employees, and 15.4% are shipping company managers. From the point of view of the maritime industry professionals, 3.3% of people have experience of 1.5,3, 11, and 12 years each while 6.7% people have experience of 4,5 and 10 years. In addition, 10% of people have experience of 2, 6,8, and 9 years while 13.3% people have experience of 1 and 7

years. Lastly, the participants worked at all six ports in an evenly distributed manner such that 12.8% of the total sample worked at each port i.e., Port Khalifa, Port Jebel Ali, Musaffah port, Mina Zayed port, Mina Rashid port, and Mina al Hamriyah port. Moreover, the sample is majorly male dominant i.e., 64.1% males and 35.9% females. The sample of participants have different ages i.e., 3.3.% of the participants are of age 20, 24,33,34,35,42,43, and 44 years. While 6.7% of each participant is aged 23,28,29,32, and 37 years, and 10% each is aged 25,26, 31, and 38 years.

Table 8.

Frequency Tables of each Descriptive

Role

		Frequency	Percent	Valid Percent	Cumulative Percent
Valid		9	23.1	23.1	23.1
	Port_employee	9	23.1	23.1	46.2
	Port_Manager	6	15.4	15.4	61.5
	Shipping_company_employee	9	23.1	23.1	84.6
	Shipping_company_manager	6	15.4	15.4	100.0
	Total	30	100.0	100.0	

Experience

		Frequency	Percent	Valid Percent	Cumulative Percent
Valid	1.00	4	10.3	13.3	13.3
	1.50	1	2.6	3.3	16.7
	2.00	3	7.7	10.0	26.7
	3.00	1	2.6	3.3	30.0
	4.00	2	5.1	6.7	36.7
	5.00	2	5.1	6.7	43.3
	6.00	3	7.7	10.0	53.3
	7.00	4	10.3	13.3	66.7
	8.00	3	7.7	10.0	76.7
	9.00	3	7.7	10.0	86.7
	10.00	2	5.1	6.7	93.3
	11.00	1	2.6	3.3	96.7
	12.00	1	2.6	3.3	100.0
	Total	30	76.9	100.0	
Missing	System	9	23.1		
Total		39	100.0		

Gender

		Frequency	Percent	Valid Percent	Cumulative Percent
Valid		9	23.1	23.1	23.1
	Female	5	35.9	35.9	35.9
	Male	25	64.1	64.1	100.0
	Total	30	100.0	100.0	

Age

		Frequency	Percent	Valid Percent	Cumulative Percent
Valid	20.00	1	2.6	3.3	3.3
	23.00	2	5.1	6.7	10.0
	24.00	1	2.6	3.3	13.3
	25.00	3	7.7	10.0	23.3
	26.00	3	7.7	10.0	33.3
	28.00	2	5.1	6.7	40.0
	29.00	2	5.1	6.7	46.7
	31.00	3	7.7	10.0	56.7
	32.00	2	5.1	6.7	63.3
	33.00	1	2.6	3.3	66.7
	34.00	1	2.6	3.3	70.0
	35.00	1	2.6	3.3	73.3
	37.00	2	5.1	6.7	80.0
	38.00	3	7.7	10.0	90.0
	42.00	1	2.6	3.3	93.3
	43.00	1	2.6	3.3	96.7
	44.00	1	2.6	3.3	100.0
	Total	30	76.9	100.0	
Total		30	100.0		

Figure 1.

Bar Graph of Role

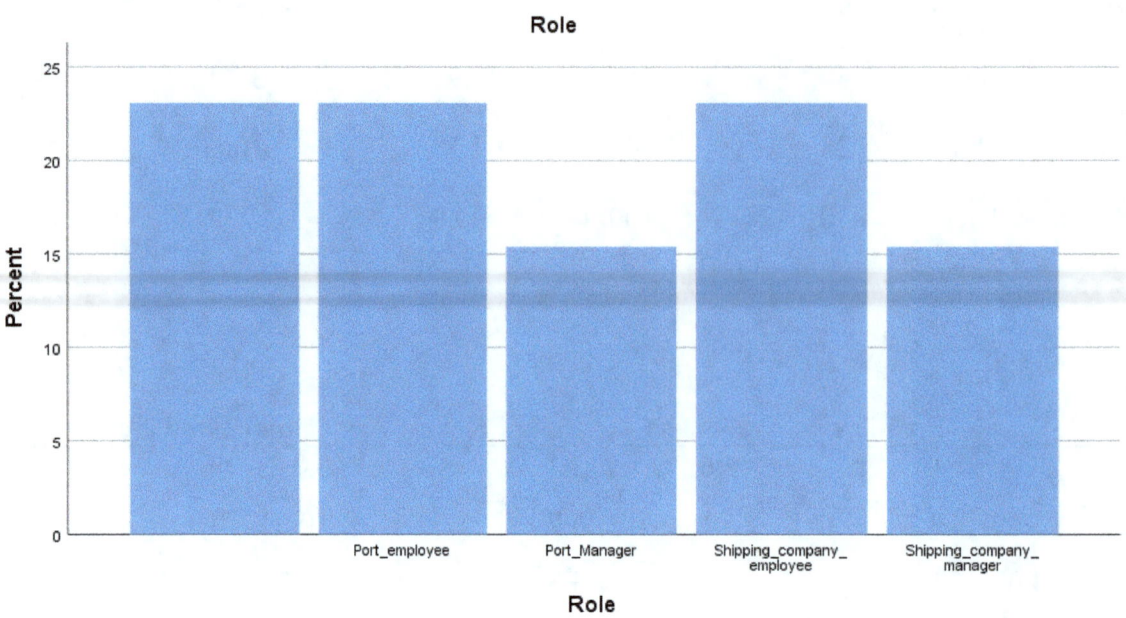

Figure 2.
Bar Graph of Years of Experience

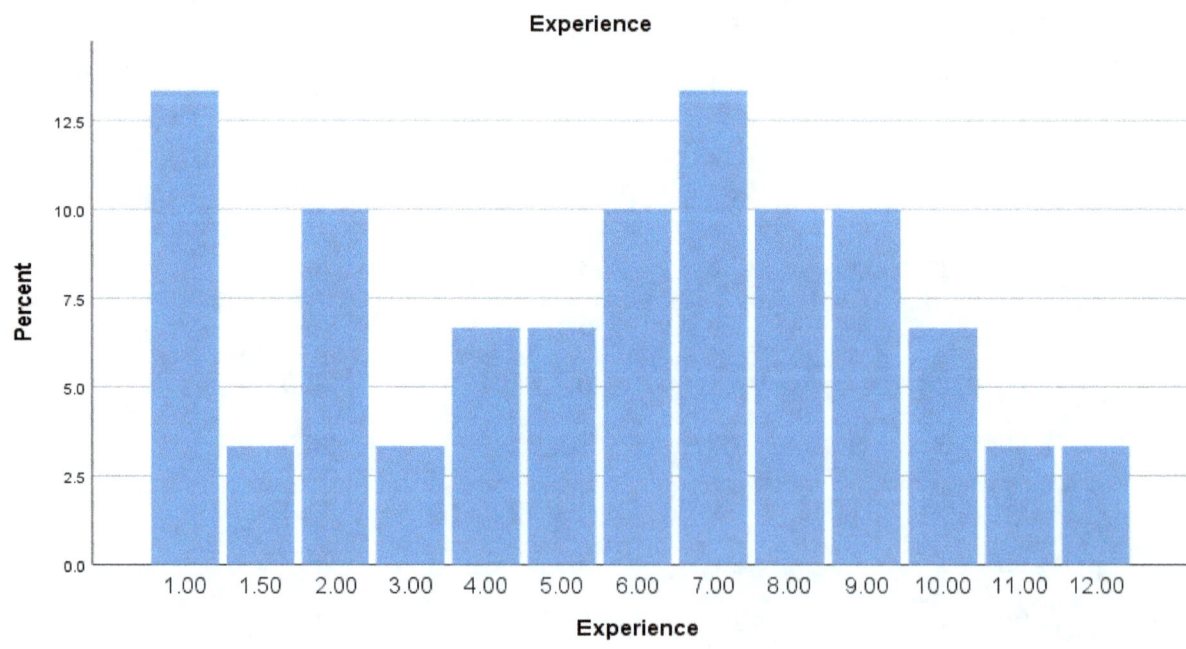

Figure 3.

Bar Graph based on Gender

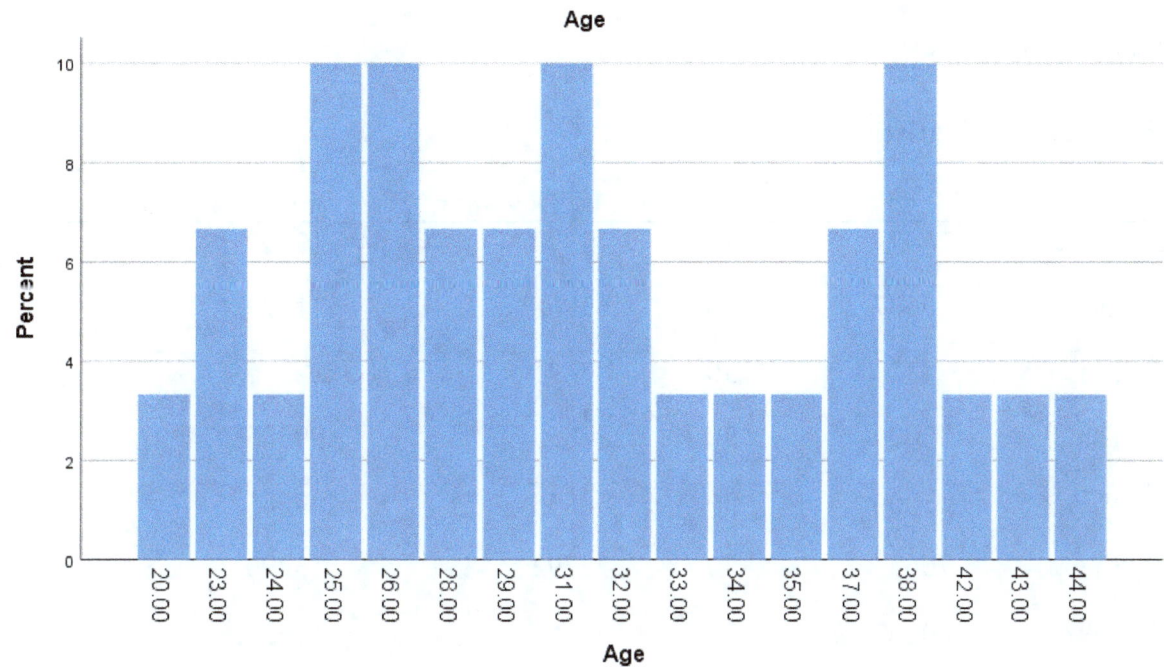

Figure 4.

Bar Graph based on Age

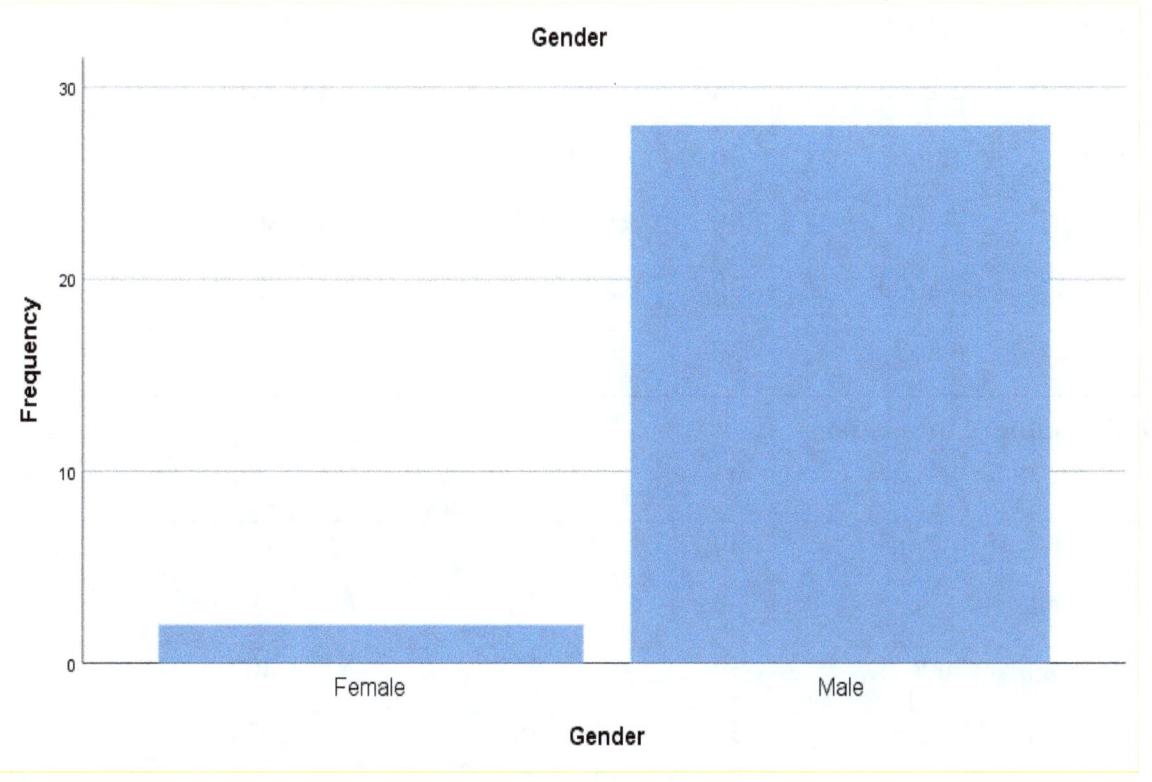

Now the primary research is focused on applying t-tests the results are shown below. The paired sample t-test is conducted on SPSS. The results are as follows:

Table 9.

Results of Paired t-test

Paired Samples Statistics

		Mean	N	Std. Deviation	Std. Error Mean
Pair 1	Indep1	.7667	30	.72793	.13290
	Dep1	3.0667	30	.63968	.11679
Pair 2	Indep4	3.4333	30	.67891	.12395
	Dep2	3.5000	30	.50855	.09285
Pair 3	Dep2	3.5000	30	.50855	.09285
	Indep1	.7667	30	.72793	.13290
Pair 4	Dep1	3.0667	30	.63968	.11679
	Indep4	3.4333	30	.67891	.12395
Pair 5	Dep1	3.0667	30	.63968	.11679
	Indep2	2.2000	30	.84690	.15462
Pair 6	Dep2	3.5000	30	.50855	.09285
	Indep2	2.2000	30	.84690	.15462
Pair 7	Dep1	3.0667	30	.63968	.11679
	Indep3	.4667	30	.62881	.11480
Pair 8	Dep2	3.5000	30	.50855	.09285
	Indep3	.4667	30	.62881	.11480

Paired Samples Correlations

		N	Correlation	Sig.
Pair 1	Indep1 & Dep1	30	-.262	.162
Pair 2	Indep4 & Dep2	30	.050	.793
Pair 3	Dep2 & Indep1	30	-.047	.807
Pair 4	Dep1 & Indep4	30	-.386	.035

		30	-.089	.640
Pair 5	Dep1 & Indep2	30	-.089	.640
Pair 6	Dep2 & Indep2	30	.000	1.000
Pair 7	Dep1 & Indep3	30	-.080	.674
Pair 8	Dep2 & Indep3	30	-.108	.571

Paired Samples Test

		Paired Differences							
					95% Confidence Interval of the Difference				Sig. (2-tailed)
		Mean	Std. Deviation	Std. Error Mean	Lower	Upper	t	df	
Pair 1	Indep1 - Dep1	-2.30000	1.08755	.19856	-2.70610	-1.89390	-11.584	29	.000
Pair 2	Indep4 - Dep2	-.06667	.82768	.15111	-.37573	.24239	-.441	29	.662
Pair 3	Dep2 - Indep1	2.73333	.90719	.16563	2.39458	3.07208	16.503	29	.000
Pair 4	Dep1 - Indep4	-.36667	1.09807	.20048	-.77669	.04336	-1.829	29	.004
Pair 5	Dep1 - Indep2	.86667	1.10589	.20191	.45372	1.27961	4.292	29	.000
Pair 6	Dep2 - Indep2	1.30000	.98786	.18036	.93113	1.66887	7.208	29	.000
Pair 7	Dep1 - Indep3	2.60000	.93218	.17019	2.25192	2.94808	15.277	29	.000
Pair 8	Dep2 - Indep3	3.03333	.85029	.15524	2.71583	3.35084	19.540	29	.000

The significance level for this primary research is 0.05 such that a value less than 0.05 means that the alternate hypothesis is true. The research findings show that the value of p is less than 0.05, which makes the alternative hypothesis true with just one deviation that vessel design is already incorporated at the ports of UAE, which is why for one pair the value of p is 0.662. This infers that there is a practical embracement of environment-friendly practices by UAE ports and shipping companies. Furthermore, there is a positive and significant impact of these initiatives on the efficiency and health of the marine environment. To further endorse and validate this hypothesis, the ANOVA test is further applied. This test is proof that solar energy, wind energy, and innovative propulsion systems have a lot of scope at UAE ports where vessel design is established at many ports such that these initiatives have a positive impact on the efficiency of the maritime energy sector in UAE ports. To attest to the findings of the t-test, the ANOVA variance test is used on the findings of a survey in the following table.

Table 10.

ANOVA test results

ANOVA

		Sum of Squares	df	Mean Square	F	Sig.
Group1	Between Groups	8.367	16	.523	1.942	.006
	Within Groups	3.500	13	.269		
	Total	11.867	29			
Group2	Between Groups	3.500	16	.219	.711	.004
	Within Groups	4.000	13	.308		
	Total	7.500	29			

The results of the ANOVA test also suggest a significant value i.e., less than 0.05, which infers that the alternate hypothesis is true. Hence, the use of green shipping practices at UAE ports has a positive impact on the efficiency of maritime energy management along with a cleaner environment.

The mean plots created by the ANOVA test for each group are as follows:

Figure 5

Mean Plots of ANOVA variance test

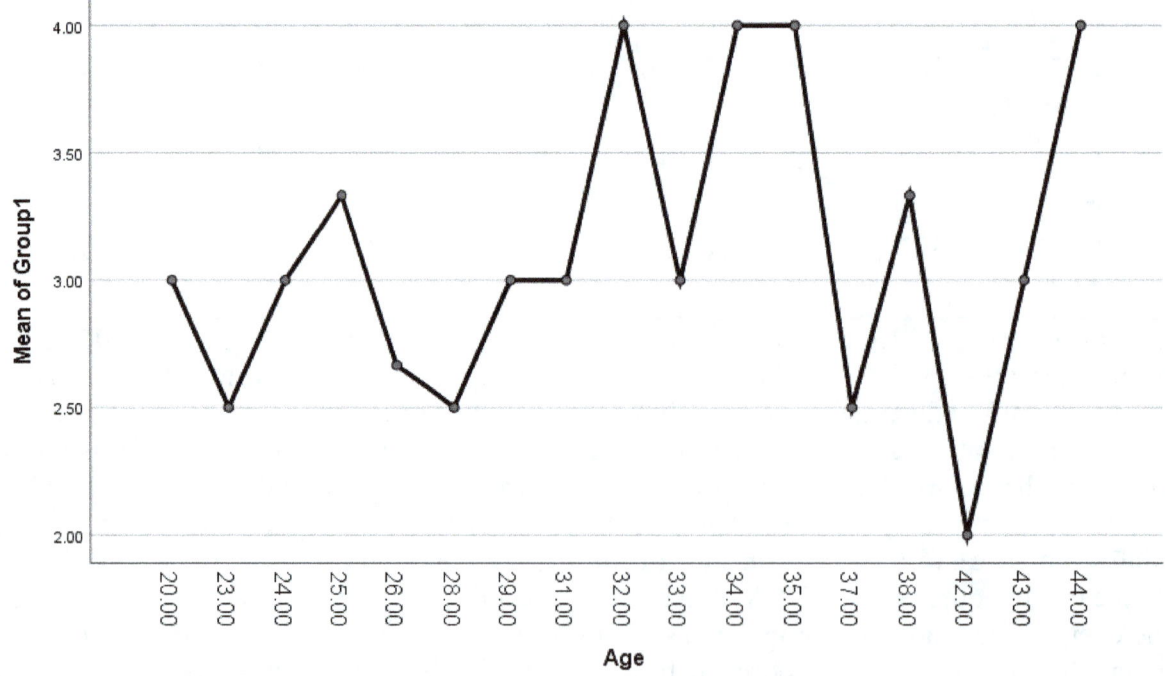

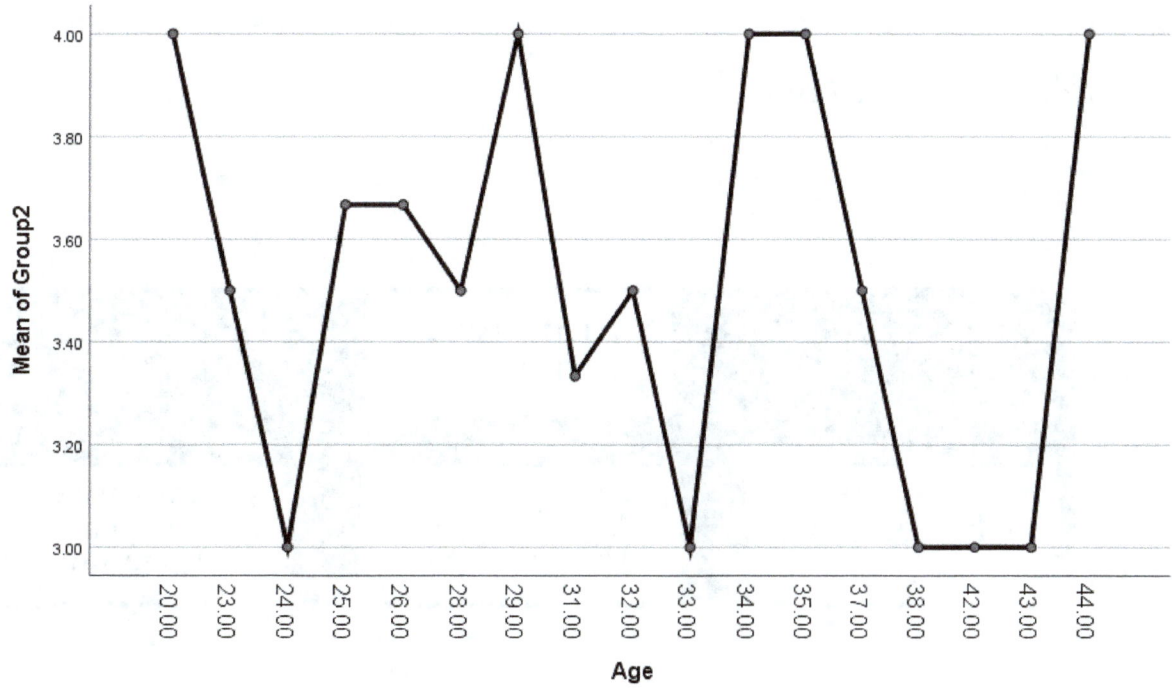

4.3.2. Thematic Categorical Coding

To gather comments from workers regarding the use of green practices in the maritime industry of UAE ports, the additional comments of three participants are used. In this case, one participant proposes the implementation of solar energy at each port in the UAE. Another participant advocates for the use of wind energy along with the incorporation of sustainable vessel design. Lastly, a participant posits that innovative propulsion systems present a viable solution that offers both efficiency and environmental sustainability within the UAE's maritime energy sector. Thus, three key themes to enhance efficiency in the maritime energy sector are solar energy, wind energy, and vessel design and innovative propulsion systems endorsed on a smaller scale by private entities at different ports per the needs of the specific area. The themes are illustrated below.

Figure 6.

Categorical Themes of the Research

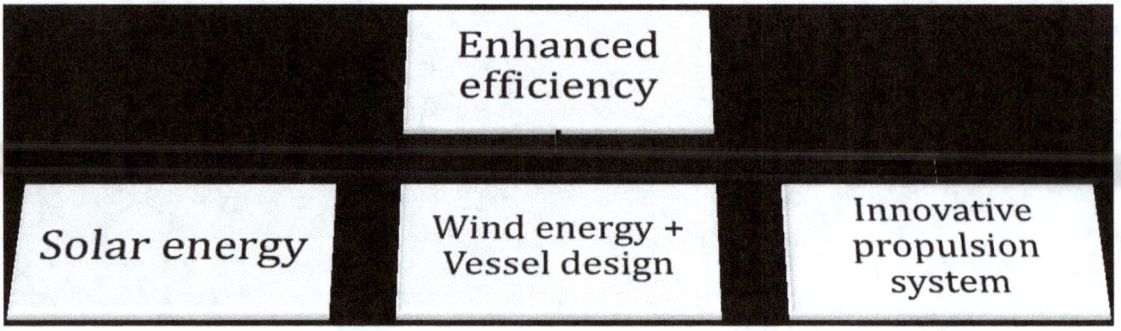

4.4. Summary

This chapter has provided key details and findings of primary research in tabular form where each of the findings is compiled and analysed. These findings have verified the alternate hypothesis as the correct one that exemplified the practical embracement of environment-friendly practices by UAE ports and shipping companies where there is a positive and significant impact of these initiatives on the efficiency and health of the marine environment. Now the following is the last chapter that envisages key discussions, conclusions, limitations, recommendations, and implications associated with the research.

Chapter 5

DISCUSSION, CONCLUSIONS, AND RECOMMENDATIONS

This chapter details the salient findings of the dissertation along with a key emphasis on primary and secondary findings. This chapter also includes recommendations and implications of the research topic in the following sections.

5.1. Interpretation of Findings

The research findings are derived from both secondary and primary research through the use of surveys among research participants that offer a comprehensive understanding of the current state of sustainable practices in the UAE maritime industry. The literature review has highlighted various facets of environmental-friendly initiatives that include solar power utilization, wind energy adoption, innovative propulsion systems, and optimised vessel design. Though individual studies have contributed valuable insights, a research gap emerged that has emphasised the need to synthesize these aspects into a holistic understanding of how diverse sustainable practices collectively contribute to the efficiency and health of the marine environment in UAE ports and shipping companies. Moreover, the research has also restated the question as to what extent are environment-friendly practices embraced by UAE ports and shipping companies, and what the collective impact of these initiatives is on the efficiency and health of the marine environment. In regards to the question, the corresponding hypotheses shifted from a null assumption of no substantial embracement or impact to an affirmative stance acknowledging practical embracement and a significantly positive impact on marine efficiency and health. This realignment of research queries aimed to guide the primary research for exploring the synergies among different sustainable initiatives along with their general influence on the UAE maritime industry along with redefining that the aim is not only to explore efficiency but to know about the short-term endorsement and the need for long-term sustainability. The question is restated owing to the key themes of the literature review and keeping that context intact, the primary research has been conducted. The research involved the use of surveys to collect data on the embracement of environment-friendly practices by UAE ports and shipping companies. For the primary study, firstly, the descriptive analysis of the participants revealed a diverse sample, with different roles, experiences, port affiliations, gender distributions, and age ranges. This diversity ensures a comprehensive representation of various stakeholders in the UAE maritime industry at Port Khalifa, Mina Zayed, Musaffah Port, Port Jebel Ali, Mina Rashid, and Mina Al Hamriyah. The survey findings from the workers at these ports were compiled and a paired sample t-test was applied. The results indicated a practical embracement of environment-friendly practices by UAE ports and shipping companies, supporting the alternative hypothesis. However, a minor deviation was noted in vessel design, where the p-value was 0.662, which suggests that this aspect is already incorporated at UAE ports. Hence, the findings supported the hypothesis of a positive and significant impact of these initiatives on the efficiency and health of the marine environment. To further validate these findings, ANOVA variance tests were applied that showed significant results with p-values less than 0.05. This reinforced the implication that solar energy, wind energy, and innovative propulsion systems have significant potential at UAE ports that contribute positively to the efficiency of maritime energy management and promote a cleaner environment. Lastly, thematic categorical coding is also done for the participants' comments that have revealed key themes to enhance efficiency in the maritime energy sector i.e., the widespread use of solar energy, wind energy, and vessel design along with the adoption of innovative propulsion systems. These themes underscored the importance of tailoring sustainable practices to the specific needs of different ports. In a nutshell, the interpretation of findings implies a positive outlook for the embracement of environment-friendly practices in the UAE maritime industry. The diverse and representative sample and rigorous statistical analyses have supported the conclusion that these practices not only find practical acceptance but also contribute significantly to the efficiency and health of the marine environment. Finally, the identified themes from participant comments provide actionable insights for stakeholders that highlight specific areas of focus like solar and wind energy, vessel design, and innovative propulsion systems that can be targeted for further enhancement of sustainability practices in the UAE maritime sector. Therefore, these findings contribute to the existing body of knowledge on sustainable practices in the maritime industry along with the provision of valuable guidance for future initiatives and policymaking in the UAE.

5.2. Limitations of the Study

Despite the valuable insights gained from this research, it is essential to acknowledge its limitations and suggest potential avenues for future research to build upon and enhance the use of sustainable practices in the UAE maritime industry. Various factors constrain the generalizability and robustness of the findings, which are the limitations that affect the scope of the study. Firstly, the research relies on a quantitative survey approach, which is efficient for large-scale data collection, but limits the depth of understanding. The survey format does not capture the nuanced perspectives and qualitative details that hinder the context for the embracement of sustainable practices in the UAE maritime sector. In this regard, future researchers should consider the incorporation of qualitative methods like interviews or focus groups to delve deeper into the motivations, challenges, and experiences of stakeholders who are involved in sustainable initiatives. Secondly, the sample size of the study is diverse, but it does not fully represent the entire population of stakeholders in the UAE maritime industry. Moreover, the research is focused on specific roles, experiences, and ports that potentially overlook certain perspectives. Thus, future researchers can conduct a more extensive and inclusive sample that covers a broader range of roles, experiences, and ports that can enhance the study's external validity and provide a more comprehensive understanding of the industry's dynamics. Another limitation of the research lies in the potential for response bias in survey-based research where participants can provide socially desirable responses or do not accurately reflect their actual practices and attitudes. In this regard, future researchers could implement additional measures like in-depth interviews or cross-validation with industry data to verify the self-reported information and ensure the reliability of the findings. Furthermore, the cross-sectional design of the study provides a snapshot of the current state of sustainable practices in the UAE maritime industry. Though it offers valuable insights into the present scenario, it does not capture the dynamics and changes over time. Hence, a longitudinal approach can help to track the evolution of sustainable practices and their impact over an extended period, which can provide a more dynamic and nuanced understanding of the industry's sustainability journey. Another limitation is that the research is primarily focused on the embracement of sustainable practices and their impact on efficiency and environmental health. However, it does not delve deeply into the economic implications of these initiatives where future researchers can explore the economic feasibility, cost-benefit analysis, and financial incentives to adopt sustainable practices in the maritime sector. They can provide a more comprehensive perspective for industry stakeholders and policymakers. Moreover, the study has assumed a positive correlation between sustainable practices and their impact on efficiency and environmental health. Though the findings support this assumption, future research can explore potential trade-offs or unintended consequences of certain sustainable initiatives. Furthermore, the conduction of comparative studies with other global maritime industries can serve as a valuable benchmark to evaluate the effectiveness of the UAE's sustainability efforts. It is important to analyse best practices and extract lessons learned from countries with established green maritime initiatives. These insights can provide valuable recommendations to enhance the long-term implementation of sustainability measures in the UAE. Finally, it is crucial to acknowledge the dynamic nature of technology and the evolving landscape of sustainability practices in the maritime industry. Continuous research becomes imperative for maritime energy managers and companies to stay abreast of emerging trends and innovations. Regular updates on the latest advancements will guarantee that the UAE maintains a leading position in sustainable practices within the maritime sector. Future researchers can direct their focus towards evaluating the effectiveness of new technologies, exploring alternative energy sources, and assessing innovative propulsion systems, contributing to a revolutionary shift in the industry's approach to sustainability. Henceforth, this research contributes valuable insights into sustainable practices in the UAE maritime industry, but it is essential to recognize its limitations and suggest avenues for future research.

5.3. Recommendations

The research on sustainable practices in the UAE maritime industry suggests several recommendations to enhance the adoption of environment-friendly initiatives and contribute to the efficiency and health of the marine environment. The first recommendation that is befitting in today's era is the integrated sustainability strategies through coordinated efforts by government and other maritime organisations that can optimise the use of energy, deriving energy, and changing the design of the ships that can reduce the carbon footprint. This holistic approach, emphasising the interconnected nature of these practices, is more likely to yield comprehensive benefits. Collaboration among ports and shipping companies at a large scale is essential to create a roadmap aligned with international sustainability standards at different ports in the UAE. Secondly, advocating for and actively engaging with regulatory bodies to establish and strengthen policies that incentivize and mandate the adoption of sustainable practices is imperative. Clear and supportive regulations can provide the maritime industry with the necessary framework and motivation to invest in green technologies, including financial incentives, tax breaks, and penalties for non-compliance. There is a need to allocate resources for continuous research and development. This helps to explore and implement the latest technologies in sustainable maritime practices. In this case, collaboration with research institutions, technology companies, and environmental organisations is important to remain at the forefront of technological advancements. It is also essential to invest in training programs and capacity-building initiatives to equip industry professionals with the skills and knowledge needed to implement and manage sustainable practices. To catalyze the advancement of a sustainable maritime industry, there is a need for strategic partnerships with educational institutions and training centers that can play a central role in creating awareness among the general public about maritime green initiatives. These collaborations can be instrumental in crafting specialized courses dedicated to green technologies, environmental conservation, and the adept operation of vessels through sustainable energy sources. In this regard, educational initiatives foster collaboration and active engagement among various stakeholders, which is imperative for future policymakers to take sustainable actions. This coalition should encompass port authorities, shipping companies, governmental bodies, and environmental organisations where the synergy among these entities is essential to create a cohesive strategy and framework for the integration of sustainable practices. An equally critical aspect involves building awareness about the manifold benefits of adopting sustainable measures within the maritime sector. This necessitates the cultivation of a shared vision among all involved parties that garners their support and commitment. Moreover, the implementation of robust monitoring and reporting systems for sustainable initiatives is paramount. This entails the establishment of key performance indicators (KPIs) to systematically track the efficiency gains and environmental impact resulting from each implemented practice. These metrics serve as a quantitative measure of success, allowing for continuous improvement and informed decision-making in the pursuit of a greener maritime future. These practices provide accountability and allow for continuous improvement and optimisation of sustainable strategies. Another aspect is to encourage the formation of collaborative industry initiatives and alliances that bring together various stakeholders. These stakeholders can share best practices, exchange knowledge, and collectively work towards common sustainability goals. To encourage the adoption of green technologies, financial incentives such as government grants, subsidies, or preferential financing for investments in solar power, wind energy, and other environmentally friendly practices are being introduced. It is also recommended to engage with local communities to ensure their concerns and perspectives in the development and implementation of sustainable practices at ports. Lastly, fostering a culture of continuous improvement and adaptation by regularly reviewing and updating sustainability strategies is vital. The maritime industry is dynamic, and technological advancements present new opportunities or challenges. Regular assessments and updates ensure that the industry remains at the forefront of sustainable practices. Therefore, by implementing these recommendations, the UAE maritime industry can not only embrace sustainable practices but also position itself as a global leader in environmentally responsible maritime operations, contributing to the health of the marine environment and enhancing the efficiency and long-term sustainability of the industry.

5.4. Implications

The implications drawn from the comprehensive research conducted on sustainable practices in the UAE maritime industry, considering both primary and secondary findings, have far-reaching effects on various facets of the industry and its stakeholders. The primary findings, derived from quantitative analysis are a manifestation of the current state of sustainability practices in UAE ports and shipping companies. The t-test results indicate a significant embracement of environment-friendly practices, except for vessel design, which is already well-incorporated into the ports of the UAE. This finding suggests that the maritime industry in the UAE has made substantial progress in adopting sustainable initiatives, affirming the shift towards cleaner and more efficient practices. The ANOVA test results reveal the significance of solar energy, wind energy, and innovative propulsion systems, signalling a considerable scope for these practices in enhancing the efficiency of maritime energy management at UAE ports. The mean plots from the ANOVA test provide a visual representation of the positive impact these practices can have on the overall efficiency of the maritime industry. The thematic categorical coding of participant comments reinforces the importance of solar energy, wind energy, vessel design, and innovative propulsion systems as key themes in enhancing efficiency within the maritime sector. These primary findings have profound implications for the UAE maritime industry. The affirmation of practical embracement of environment-friendly practices is a testament to the industry's commitment to sustainability. It not only signifies a positive shift in the mindset of port authorities and shipping companies but also suggests a recognition of the critical role the industry plays in environmental conservation. The positive impact on the efficiency and health of the marine environment implies that the industry's efforts are not merely symbolic but translate into tangible benefits. These benefits are for both business operations and the ecological well-being of the maritime ecosystem. Moreover, the finding that vessel design is already well-integrated offers an opportunity for the industry to showcase this success and potentially serve as a benchmark for other regions. The secondary findings derived from the literature review add depth and context to the primary findings. The identification of a research gap in the literature underscores the novelty and significance of the current study. The shift in the research question and hypothesis to address this gap reflects a nuanced understanding of the intricacies involved in synthesizing various sustainable practices. The recommendations derived from the synthesis of primary and secondary findings are grounded in both empirical evidence and theoretical frameworks, enhancing their practical relevance. In terms of intuition, the findings imply that the UAE maritime industry is on a positive trajectory towards becoming a sustainable and environmentally responsible sector. The embracement of sustainable practices suggests a forward-thinking approach, aligning with global efforts to mitigate the environmental impact of maritime activities. The emphasis on established green initiatives aligns with the broader trends in the global maritime industry, indicating that the UAE is not only keeping pace with international standards but, in some aspects, leading the way. The implications extend beyond the industry itself. As the UAE is a major player in international trade and shipping, the adoption of sustainable practices sends a powerful signal to the global community. It positions the UAE as a responsible and environmentally conscious hub for maritime activities, potentially influencing other regions to follow suit. In conclusion, the implications of the research findings are multi-faceted. They signify a positive shift towards sustainability in the UAE maritime industry, with practical embracement of green practices and a measurable impact on efficiency and environmental health. These findings contribute not only to the local industry but also have broader implications for global maritime practices and environmental conservation efforts. The recommendations derived from the study provide actionable steps for further improvement, ensuring a continuous journey towards a more sustainable and resilient maritime sector in the UAE.

5.5. Conclusion

In conclusion, the research on sustainable practices in the UAE maritime industry presents a holistic and nuanced understanding of the current state of environmental consciousness and efficiency within the sector. The journey through secondary literature and primary data collection has unveiled a landscape where the industry is not only embracing sustainable initiatives but is making significant strides towards integrating them into its core operations. The revised research question, shaped by a critical analysis of existing literature, brought attention to a research gap that needed to be addressed: the lack of a comprehensive synthesis of various sustainable practices and their collective impact on the efficiency and health of the marine environment in UAE ports. This realignment of focus, captured in the restated question and hypotheses, guided the research toward investigating the interconnected nature of these practices. The quantitative research design is empirical evidence that is gathered by the use of a robust framework for assessing the embracement levels of environment-friendly practices by UAE ports and shipping companies. In addition to quantitative findings, the descriptive analysis of the participants ensured a representative sample that added depth to the quantitative findings. The paired sample t-test scrutinized the mean differences, revealing a remarkable embracement of sustainable practices, with vessel design being the exception due to its already established status. The ANOVA variance test is like an attested inference that suggests the implementation of green initiatives at a smaller scale along with a need for long-term implementation for the increased efficiency of maritime energy management. These primary findings, complemented by secondary insights from the literature review, offer a comprehensive snapshot of the UAE maritime industry's commitment to sustainable practices. The recommendations derived from the synthesis of primary and secondary findings provide a roadmap for further improvement, emphasising the need for integrated sustainability strategies, policy advocacy, research and development, capacity building, stakeholder engagement, and continuous improvement. These recommendations are not only grounded in empirical evidence but also informed by theoretical frameworks, ensuring practical relevance and feasibility. The implications drawn from the research are profound. They suggest that the UAE maritime industry is not merely paying lip service to sustainability but is actively transforming its operational landscape. The embracement of environment-friendly practices signifies a paradigm shift, where industry players are acknowledging their role in environmental conservation and taking tangible steps towards a greener future. The positive impact on the efficiency and health of the marine environment resonates beyond the industry, positioning the UAE as a responsible global player in maritime activities. The secondary findings from the literature review, coupled with the primary research insights, highlight the novelty and significance of this study. The identification of a research gap and the subsequent realignment of the research question demonstrate a scholarly approach to knowledge creation, contributing not only to the local understanding of the industry but also enriching the global discourse on sustainable maritime practices. Intuitively, these findings suggest that the UAE maritime industry is on a trajectory toward becoming a benchmark for sustainability in the global maritime arena. The emphasis on solar and wind energy, innovative propulsion systems, and optimised vessel design aligns with global trends, positioning the UAE as not just a follower but a leader in environmental consciousness within the maritime sector. In essence, this research is not merely an academic exercise; it is a testament to the transformative potential of industry-wide commitment to sustainability. The UAE maritime industry's journey, as illuminated by this study, acts as a motivation and inspiration for other regions grappling with the environmental consequences of maritime activities. The recommendations, if implemented, can propel the industry further along this trajectory, ensuring a future where efficiency and environmental responsibility coexist seamlessly. Hence, in the navigation of the complex waters of environmental stewardship, the findings and recommendations of this research provide a compass for the UAE maritime industry. It is a call to action, urging the industry to not only celebrate its successes but to continuously strive for improvement, adaptability, and a harmonious coexistence with the marine environment.

REFERENCES

Abou Kasm, O., Diabat, A., & Bierlaire, M. (2021). Vessel scheduling with pilotage and tugging considerations. *Transportation Research Part E: Logistics and Transportation Review*, *148*, 102231. https://doi.org/10.1016/j.tre.2021.102231

Akhavan, M. (2019). 7. Gateway: Revisiting Dubai as a Port City. In *7. Gateway: Revisiting Dubai as a Port City* (pp. 175–193). New York University Press. https://doi.org/10.18574/nyu/9781479880010.003.0008

Akhavan, M. (2020). Economic Diversification, Freight Flows and Transnational Expansion in Dubai Hub Port-City. In M. Akhavan (Ed.), *Port Geography and Hinterland Development Dynamics: Insights from Major Port-cities of the Middle East* (pp. 71–114). Springer International Publishing. https://doi.org/10.1007/978-3-030-52578-1_5

Al Jaberi, N. H. (2019). UNITED ARAB EMIRATES POST OIL STRATEGY: AN EXAMINATION OF DIVERSIFICATION STRATEGIES AND CHALLENGES. *Theses*. https://scholarworks.uaeu.ac.ae/all_theses/851

Alblooshi, E., & Ebrahim, Z. (2022). Measuring the impact of port operations on economic development of developing countries. *Journal of Tianjin University Science and Technology*, *55*(5).

Alketbi, M. S. A. H. (2023). *Sustainable development: Influence of economic decisions taken at the state level in the United Arab Emirates (UAE)*. https://uobrep.openrepository.com/handle/10547/625941

Almeida, F. (2023). Challenges in the Digital Transformation of Ports. *Businesses*, *3*(4), Article 4. https://doi.org/10.3390/businesses3040034

Alsubal, S., Alaloul, W. S., Shawn, E. L., Liew, M. S., Palaniappan, P., & Musarat, M. A. (2021). Life Cycle Cost Assessment of Offshore Wind Farm: Kudat Malaysia Case. *Sustainability*, *13*(14), Article 14. https://doi.org/10.3390/su13147943

An, H., Bahamaish, F., & Lee, D.-W. (2021). Simulation and Optimisation for a Closed-Loop Vessel Dispatching Problem in the Middle East Considering Various Uncertainties. *Applied Sciences*, *11*(20), Article 20. https://doi.org/10.3390/app11209626

Arun Kumar, S. V. V., Nagababu, G., Sharma, R., & Kumar, R. (2020). Synergetic use of multiple scatterometers for offshore wind energy potential assessment. *Ocean Engineering*, *196*, 106745. https://doi.org/10.1016/j.oceaneng.2019.106745

Ash, N., & Scarbrough, T. (2019). *Sailing on Solar—Could green ammonia decarbonise international shipping?*

Ball, H. L. (2019). Conducting online surveys. *Journal of Human Lactation*, *35*(3), 413–417.

Bapte, V. D., & Bejalwar, S. A. (2021). Promoting the Use of Reference Management Tools An Opportunity for Librarians to Promote Scientific Tradition. *DESIDOC Journal of*

Library & Information Technology, *42*(1), 64–70.
https://doi.org/10.14429/djlit.42.1.17251

Bax, N., Novaglio, C., Maxwell, K. H., Meyers, K., McCann, J., Jennings, S., Frusher, S.,
Fulton, E. A., Nursey-Bray, M., Fischer, M., Anderson, K., Layton, C., Emad, G. R.,
Alexander, K. A., Rousseau, Y., Lunn, Z., & Carter, C. G. (2022). Ocean resource
use: Building the coastal blue economy. *Reviews in Fish Biology and Fisheries*, *32*(1),
189–207. https://doi.org/10.1007/s11160-021-09636-0

Belibassakis, K., Bleuanus, S., Vermeiden, J., & Townsend, N. (2021, June 20). *Combined
performance of innovative biomimetic ship propulsion system in waves with Dual
Fuel ship engine and application to short-sea shipping*. The 31st International Ocean
and Polar Engineering Conference. https://dx.doi.org/

Benamara, H., Hoffmann, J., & Youssef, F. (2019). Maritime Transport: The Sustainability
Imperative. In H. N. Psaraftis (Ed.), *Sustainable Shipping: A Cross-Disciplinary View*
(pp. 1–31). Springer International Publishing. https://doi.org/10.1007/978-3-030-
04330-8_1

Bhat, S., Antony, J., Maalouf, M., E.V., G., & Salah, S. (2023). Applications of six sigma for
service quality enhancement in the UAE: A multiple case study analysis and lessons
learned. *International Journal of Lean Six Sigma*, *14*(7), 1492–1517.
https://doi.org/10.1108/IJLSS-06-2022-0144

Bloomfield, J., & Fisher, M. J. (2019). Quantitative research design. *Journal of the
Australasian Rehabilitation Nurses Association*, *22*(2), 27–30.

Buonomano, A., Del Papa, G., Giuzio, G. F., Palombo, A., & Russo, G. (2023). Future
pathways for decarbonization and energy efficiency of ports: Modelling and
optimisation as sustainable energy hubs. *Journal of Cleaner Production*, *420*, 138389.
https://doi.org/10.1016/j.jclepro.2023.138389

Chaudhuri, A., Datta, R., Kumar, M. P., Davim, J. P., & Pramanik, S. (2022). Energy
Conversion Strategies for Wind Energy System: Electrical, Mechanical and Material
Aspects. *Materials*, *15*(3), Article 3. https://doi.org/10.3390/ma15031232

Chua, J. Y., Wang, X., & Yuen, K. F. (2023). Sustainable shipping management: Definitions,
critical success factors, drivers and performance. *Transport Policy*, *141*, 72–82.
https://doi.org/10.1016/j.tranpol.2023.07.012

Clemente, D., Cabral, T., Rosa-Santos, P., & Taveira-Pinto, F. (2023). Blue Seaports: The
Smart, Sustainable and Electrified Ports of the Future. *Smart Cities*, *6*(3), Article 3.
https://doi.org/10.3390/smartcities6030074

Coimbatore Meenakshi Sundaram, A., & Karimi, I. A. (2023). Sustainability Analysis of an
LNG Bunkering Protocol. *ACS Sustainable Chemistry & Engineering*.
https://doi.org/10.1021/acssuschemeng.3c02914

de Kat, J. O., & Mouawad, J. (2019). Green ship technologies. *Sustainable Shipping: A Cross-Disciplinary View*, 33–92.

de la Peña Zarzuelo, I., Soeane, M. J. F., & Bermúdez, B. L. (2020). Industry 4.0 in the port and maritime industry: A literature review. *Journal of Industrial Information Integration*, *20*, 100173.

Delios, A., Clemente, E. G., Wu, T., Tan, H., Wang, Y., Gordon, M., Viganola, D., Chen, Z., Dreber, A., & Johannesson, M. (2022). Examining the generalizability of research findings from archival data. *Proceedings of the National Academy of Sciences*, *119*(30), e2120377119.

Dewan, M. H., & Godina, R. (2023). Roles and challenges of seafarers for implementation of energy efficiency operational measures onboard ships. *Marine Policy*, *155*, 105746. https://doi.org/10.1016/j.marpol.2023.105746

Diaz, S., Al Hammadi, N., El Nasr, A. S., Villasuso, F., Prakash, S., Baobaid, O., Gracias, D., & Mills, R. (2023, October 2). *Green Corridor: A Feasible Option for the UAE Decarbonization Pathway, Opportunities & Challenges*. ADIPEC. https://doi.org/10.2118/216033-MS

Elnajjar, H. M., Shehata, A. S., Elbatran, A. H. A., & Shehadeh, M. F. (2021). Experimental and techno-economic feasibility analysis of renewable energy technologies for Jabel Ali Port in UAE. *Energy Reports*, *7*, 116–136. https://doi.org/10.1016/j.egyr.2021.08.102

Fandi, O. M., Dol, S. S., & Alavi, M. (2022). Review of Renewable Energy Applications and Feasibility of Tidal Energy in the United Arab Emirates. *Renewable Energy Research and Applications*, *3*(2), 165–174. https://doi.org/10.22044/rera.2022.11747.1107

Farrukh, A., Mathrani, S., & Sajjad, A. (2023). An exploratory study of green-lean-six sigma motivators for environmental sustainability: Managerial insights from a developed and developing economy. *Business Strategy and the Environment*, *n/a*(n/a). https://doi.org/10.1002/bse.3412

Formaneck, S. (2019). A STUDY OF SUSTAINABLE FACILITIES MANAGEMENT FROM A GREEN SUPPLY CHAIN PERSPECTIVE IN THE UNITED ARAB EMIRATES. *Journal of Turkish Operations Management*, *3*(2), Article 2.

Fraga-Lamas, P., Fernández-Caramés, T. M., Fraga-Lamas, P., & Fernández-Caramés, T. M. (2020). Leveraging Blockchain for Sustainability and Open Innovation: A Cyber-Resilient Approach toward EU Green Deal and UN Sustainable Development Goals. In *Computer Security Threats*. IntechOpen. https://doi.org/10.5772/intechopen.92371

Garcia, B., Foerster, A., & Lin, J. (2021). Net Zero for the International Shipping Sector? An Analysis of the Implementation and Regulatory Challenges of the IMO Strategy on Reduction of GHG Emissions. *Journal of Environmental Law*, *33*(1), 85–112. https://doi.org/10.1093/jel/eqaa014

Gerald, B. (2018). A brief review of independent, dependent and one sample t-test. *International Journal of Applied Mathematics and Theoretical Physics*, *4*(2), 50–54.

Gisle, T. (2023). *Navigating Past the Crucible and into the Blue: The Water Energy Nexus: The bold plan signed by Israel, Jordan and the UAE addressing climate, peace and trade. Can the promise of a better future really be wrested from the clutches of past conflict in the Middle East?* https://urn.kb.se/resolve?urn=urn:nbn:se:su:diva-220786

Gras, S. (2013). *Hierarchical information retreival and boolean search strings* (United States Patent US20130091113A1). https://patents.google.com/patent/US20130091113A1/en

Holian, R., & Coghlan, D. (2013). Ethical issues and role duality in insider action research: Challenges for action research degree programmes. *Systemic Practice and Action Research*, *26*, 399–415.

Holmes, A. G. D. (2020). Researcher Positionality—A Consideration of Its Influence and Place in Qualitative Research—A New Researcher Guide. *Shanlax International Journal of Education*, *8*(4), 1–10.

Hughes, A. C., Orr, M. C., Ma, K., Costello, M. J., Waller, J., Provoost, P., Yang, Q., Zhu, C., & Qiao, H. (2021). Sampling biases shape our view of the natural world. *Ecography*, *44*(9), 1259–1269.

Ikpogu, N. (2021). Barriers to Technology Adoption Among Maritime Industry Stakeholders in Nigeria. *Walden Dissertations and Doctoral Studies*. https://scholarworks.waldenu.edu/dissertations/10805

IMO. (2019). *IMO GHG studies*. https://www.imo.org/en/OurWork/Environment/Pages/IMO-GHG-studies.aspx

Jan, A. A., Lai, F.-W., Draz, M. U., Tahir, M., Ali, S. E. A., Zahid, M., & Shad, M. K. (2022). Integrating sustainability practices into islamic corporate governance for sustainable firm performance: From the lens of agency and stakeholder theories. *Quality & Quantity*, *56*(5), 2989–3012. https://doi.org/10.1007/s11135-021-01261-0

Jelić, M., Mrzljak, V., Radica, G., & Račić, N. (2021). An alternative and hybrid propulsion for merchant ships: Current state and perspective. *Energy Sources, Part A: Recovery, Utilization, and Environmental Effects*, *0*(0), 1–33. https://doi.org/10.1080/15567036.2021.1963354

Joubi, A., Akimoto, Y., & Okajima, K. (2022). A Production and Delivery Model of Hydrogen from Solar Thermal Energy in the United Arab Emirates. *Energies*, *15*(11), Article 11. https://doi.org/10.3390/en15114000

Jović, M., Tijan, E., Žgaljić, D., & Aksentijević, S. (2020). Improving maritime transport sustainability using blockchain-based information exchange. *Sustainability*, *12*(21), 8866.

Kandiyil, D. R. (2022). Use of Marine Renewable Energy in Ports of Middle East: A Step Toward Sustainable Ports. In E. Heggy, V. Bermudez, & M. Vermeersch (Eds.), *Sustainable Energy-Water-Environment Nexus in Deserts* (pp. 349–356). Springer International Publishing. https://doi.org/10.1007/978-3-030-76081-6_42

Kardzhilov, Y. N. (2023). *Internal and External Drivers in Voluntary and Coercive Adoption of Green Supply Chain Practices in the Maritime Industry* [Master thesis, University of South-Eastern Norway]. https://openarchive.usn.no/usn-xmlui/handle/11250/3079967

Kechagias, E. P., Chatzistelios, G., Papadopoulos, G. A., & Apostolou, P. (2022). Digital transformation of the maritime industry: A cybersecurity systemic approach. *International Journal of Critical Infrastructure Protection*, *37*, 100526. https://doi.org/10.1016/j.ijcip.2022.100526

Kekeh, M., Akpinar-Elci, M., & Allen, M. J. (2020). Sea Level Rise and Coastal Communities. In R. Akhtar (Ed.), *Extreme Weather Events and Human Health: International Case Studies* (pp. 171–184). Springer International Publishing. https://doi.org/10.1007/978-3-030-23773-8_12

Ketbi, E. A. (2020). Contemporary Shifts in UAE Foreign Policy: From the Liberation of Kuwait to the Abraham Accords. *Israel Journal of Foreign Affairs*, *14*(3), 391–398. https://doi.org/10.1080/23739770.2020.1845067

Khan, M. S., & Al Marashda, S. (2023, October 2). *UAE's First Wind Energy Project— ADNOC Logistics & Roll Group partnership and Barges Solution for Offshore Breakbulk Challenges*. ADIPEC. https://doi.org/10.2118/217041-MS

Kim, H.-Y. (2014). Analysis of variance (ANOVA) comparing means of more than two groups. *Restorative Dentistry & Endodontics*, *39*(1), 74–77.

Kim, K., Roh, G., Kim, W., & Chun, K. (2020). A Preliminary Study on an Alternative Ship Propulsion System Fueled by Ammonia: Environmental and Economic Assessments. *Journal of Marine Science and Engineering*, *8*(3), Article 3. https://doi.org/10.3390/jmse8030183

Koilo, V. (2019). Sustainability issues in maritime transport and main challenges of the shipping industry. *Environmental Economics*, *10*, 48–65. https://doi.org/10.21511/ee.10(1).2019.04

Korberg, A. D., Brynolf, S., Grahn, M., & Skov, I. R. (2021). Techno-economic assessment of advanced fuels and propulsion systems in future fossil-free ships. *Renewable and Sustainable Energy Reviews*, *142*, 110861. https://doi.org/10.1016/j.rser.2021.110861

Krzymowski, A. (2020). Sustainable Development Goals in Arab Region – United Arab Emirates' Case Study. *Problemy Ekorozwoju*, *Vol. 15*(nr 1). http://yadda.icm.edu.pl/baztech/element/bwmeta1.element.baztech-0e8d004d-de14-4229-a672-3131bacff8ac

Krzymowski, A. (2022). Energy Transformation and the UAE Green Economy: Trade Exchange and Relations with Three Seas Initiative Countries. *Energies*, *15*(22), Article 22. https://doi.org/10.3390/en15228410

Lam, J. S. L., & Li, K. X. (2019). Green port marketing for sustainable growth and development. *Transport Policy*, *84*, 73–81. https://doi.org/10.1016/j.tranpol.2019.04.011

Leipold, S., Feindt, P. H., Winkel, G., & Keller, R. (2019). Discourse analysis of environmental policy revisited: Traditions, trends, perspectives. *Journal of Environmental Policy & Planning*, *21*(5), 445–463. https://doi.org/10.1080/1523908X.2019.1660462

Li, D., Xin, X., & Zhou, S. (2023). Integrated governance of the Yangtze River Delta port cluster using niche theory: A case study of Shanghai Port and Ningbo-Zhoushan Port. *Ocean & Coastal Management*, *234*, 106474. https://doi.org/10.1016/j.ocecoaman.2022.106474

Li, L., & Zhou, H. (2021). A survey of blockchain with applications in maritime and shipping industry. *Information Systems and E-Business Management*, *19*(3), 789–807. https://doi.org/10.1007/s10257-020-00480-6

Lidour, K., & Beech, M. J. (2020). At the dawn of Arabian fisheries: Fishing activities of the inhabitants of the Neolithic tripartite house of Marawah Island, Abu Dhabi Emirate (United Arab Emirates). *Arabian Archaeology and Epigraphy*, *31*(1), 140–150. https://doi.org/10.1111/aae.12134

Livsey, J. R. (2019). *ECONOMIC DIVERSIFICATION THROUGH A KNOWLEDGE-BASED ECONOMY IN THE UNITED ARAB EMIRATES: A STUDY OF PROGRESS TOWARD VISION 2021*. Monterey, CA; Naval Postgraduate School.

Mahdy, M. Y. M. (2020). *Assessment of offshore wind energy potential in the Middle East: Case studies Egypt, Arabian Peninsula* [Phd, University of Southampton]. https://eprints.soton.ac.uk/475982/

McCarney, J. (2020). Evolution in the Engine Room: A Review of Technologies to Deliver Decarbonised, Sustainable Shipping : Technology options for the shipping sector to meet international ship emissions limits. *Johnson Matthey Technology Review*, *64*(3), 374–392. https://doi.org/10.1595/205651320X15924055217177

Meicun, R. Z., Lin. (2022). Sino-Arabian Economic and Cultural Exchanges From the 8th to the 15th Centuries. In *The World of the Ancient Silk Road*. Routledge.

Mengist, W., Soromessa, T., & Legese, G. (2020). Method for conducting systematic literature review and meta-analysis for environmental science research. *MethodsX*, *7*, 100777. https://doi.org/10.1016/j.mex.2019.100777

Miller, R. L. (2015). Rogers' innovation diffusion theory (1962, 1995). In *Information seeking behaviour and technology adoption: Theories and trends* (pp. 261–274). IGI Global.

Mishra, P., Singh, U., Pandey, C. M., Mishra, P., & Pandey, G. (2019). Application of student's t-test, analysis of variance, and covariance. *Annals of Cardiac Anaesthesia, 22*(4), 407.

Mneimneh, F., Ghazzawi, H., Abu Hejjeh, M., Manganelli, M., & Ramakrishna, S. (2023). Roadmap to Achieving Sustainable Development via Green Hydrogen. *Energies, 16*(3), Article 3. https://doi.org/10.3390/en16031368

Najini, H., Nour, M., Al-Zuhair, S., & Ghaith, F. (2020). Techno-Economic Analysis of Green Building Codes in United Arab Emirates Based on a Case Study Office Building. *Sustainability, 12*(21), Article 21. https://doi.org/10.3390/su12218773

Narlikar, A. (2021). Holding up a mirror to the World Trade Organisation: Lessons from the COVID-19 pandemic. *Global Perspectives, 2*(1), 24069.

Nguyen, H. P., Hoang, A. T., Nizetic, S., Nguyen, X. P., Le, A. T., Luong, C. N., Chu, V. D., & Pham, V. V. (2021). The electric propulsion system as a green solution for management strategy of CO2 emission in ocean shipping: A comprehensive review. *International Transactions on Electrical Energy Systems, 31*(11), e12580. https://doi.org/10.1002/2050-7038.12580

Nguyen Minh, Q., Sadiq, R., & Gucma, L. (2021). Simulation-Based Performance Assessment Framework for Optimising Port Investment. *Journal of Waterway, Port, Coastal, and Ocean Engineering, 147*(4), 04021010. https://doi.org/10.1061/(ASCE)WW.1943-5460.0000640

Nuchturee, C., Li, T., & Xia, H. (2020). Energy efficiency of integrated electric propulsion for ships – A review. *Renewable and Sustainable Energy Reviews, 134*, 110145. https://doi.org/10.1016/j.rser.2020.110145

Nwaigwe, K. N., Mutabilwa, P., & Dintwa, E. (2019). An overview of solar power (PV systems) integration into electricity grids. *Materials Science for Energy Technologies, 2*(3), 629–633. https://doi.org/10.1016/j.mset.2019.07.002

Okagbue, H. I., Oguntunde, P. E., Obasi, E. C., & Akhmetshin, E. M. (2021). Trends and usage pattern of SPSS and Minitab Software in Scientific research. *Journal of Physics: Conference Series, 1734*(1), 012017.

Parmentola, A., Petrillo, A., Tutore, I., & De Felice, F. (2022). Is blockchain able to enhance environmental sustainability? A systematic review and research agenda from the perspective of Sustainable Development Goals (SDGs). *Business Strategy and the Environment, 31*(1), 194–217. https://doi.org/10.1002/bse.2882

Power, T. (2024). Human–Environment Interactions in the United Arab Emirates: An Archaeological Perspective. In J. A. Burt (Ed.), *A Natural History of the Emirates* (pp. 673–702). Springer Nature Switzerland. https://doi.org/10.1007/978-3-031-37397-8_22

Quinlan, E. R. (2008). Diffusion of Innovations. In *An Integrated Approach to Communication Theory and Research* (2nd ed.). Routledge.

Rachmawati, M., Nugroho, F. J., Supriyanto, E. E., Saksono, H., Cahyo, A. N., Natalia, F., Silviana, S., & Windy, E. (2021). *ICLSSEE 2021: Proceedings of the 1st International Conference on Law, Social Science, Economics, and Education, ICLSSEE 2021, March 6th 2021, Jakarta, Indonesia*. European Alliance for Innovation.

Ramachandran, T., Mourad, A.-H. I., & Hamed, F. (2022). A Review on Solar Energy Utilization and Projects: Development in and around the UAE. *Energies, 15*(10), Article 10. https://doi.org/10.3390/en15103754

Salem, S. B., & Jagadeesan, P. (2022). Food supply chain in pandemic, geopolitical, and climate change era—Efforts of United Arab Emirates (UAE). *agriRxiv, 2022*, 20220193858. https://doi.org/10.31220/agriRxiv.2022.00142

Salimi, M., Hosseinpour, M., & N. Borhani, T. (2022). Analysis of Solar Energy Development Strategies for a Successful Energy Transition in the UAE. *Processes, 10*(7), Article 7. https://doi.org/10.3390/pr10071338

Scells, H., Zuccon, G., Koopman, B., & Clark, J. (2020). Automatic boolean query formulation for systematic review literature search. *Proceedings of the Web Conference 2020*, 1071–1081. https://doi.org/10.1145/3366423.3380185

Shadab, S. (2019). Economic diversification and the role of non-oil sector in the united arab emirates. *Asian Journal of Multidimensional Research (AJMR), 8*(7), 65–76. http://dx.doi.org/10.5958/2278-4853.2019.00249.0

Siegel, F. R. (2019). *Adaptations of Coastal Cities to Global Warming, Sea Level Rise, Climate Change and Endemic Hazards*. Springer.

Skjærseth, J. B., Hansen, T., Donner-Amnell, J., Hanson, J., Inderberg, T. H. J., Nielsen, H. Ø., Nygaard, B., & Steen, M. (2023). *Wind Power Policies and Diffusion in the Nordic Countries: Comparative Patterns*. Springer Nature.

Smith, L. H. (2020). Selection mechanisms and their consequences: Understanding and addressing selection bias. *Current Epidemiology Reports, 7*, 179–189.

Somorin, T., Sowale, A., Shemfe, M., Ayodele, A. S., & Kolios, A. (2019). Clean Technologies and Innovation in Energy. In S. Adesola & F. Brennan (Eds.), *Energy in Africa: Policy, Management and Sustainability* (pp. 149–197). Springer International Publishing. https://doi.org/10.1007/978-3-319-91301-8_7

Spiegel-Feld, D., Wyman, K. M., & Coughlin, J. J. (2023). *Global Sustainable Cities: City Governments and Our Environmental Future*. NYU Press.

Subraelu, P., Sefelnasr, A., Sherif, M., Ebraheem, A., Kakani, N. R., & A, R. (2022). *Global Warming Climate Change and Sea Level Rise: Impact on Land Use Land Cover Features along UAE coast through Remote Sensing and GIS. 12*, 1000329. https://doi.org/10.4172/2157-7625.1000329

UNEP. (2019). *United Arab Emirates | Climate & Clean Air Coalition.* https://www.ccacoalition.org/partners/united-arab-emirates

Vairetti, C., González-Ramírez, R. G., Maldonado, S., Álvarez, C., & Voβ, S. (2019). Facilitating conditions for successful adoption of inter-organisational information systems in seaports. *Transportation Research Part A: Policy and Practice, 130*, 333–350. https://doi.org/10.1016/j.tra.2019.09.017

Viswanathan, H. S. (2022). *Coastal Tourism Sustainability in Abu Dhabi, United Arab Emirates: Environment, Protected Areas, and Culture*. University of Washington.

Walker, T. R., Adebambo, O., Del Aguila Feijoo, M. C., Elhaimer, E., Hossain, T., Edwards, S. J., Morrison, C. E., Romo, J., Sharma, N., Taylor, S., & Zomorodi, S. (2019). Chapter 27—Environmental Effects of Marine Transportation. In C. Sheppard (Ed.), *World Seas: An Environmental Evaluation (Second Edition)* (pp. 505–530). Academic Press. https://doi.org/10.1016/B978-0-12-805052-1.00030-9

Wang, C., & Wang, L. (2023). Green investment and vertical alliances in the maritime supply chain. *Environment, Development and Sustainability, 25*(7), 6657–6687. https://doi.org/10.1007/s10668-022-02322-6

Wang, X., Yuen, K. F., Wong, Y. D., & Li, K. X. (2020). How can the maritime industry meet Sustainable Development Goals? An analysis of sustainability reports from the social entrepreneurship perspective. *Transportation Research Part D: Transport and Environment, 78*, 102173. https://doi.org/10.1016/j.trd.2019.11.002

Yang, C.-S., & Lin, M. S.-M. (2023). The impact of digitalization and digital logistics platform adoption on organisational performance in maritime logistics of Taiwan. *Maritime Policy & Management, 0*(0), 1–18. https://doi.org/10.1080/03088839.2023.2234911

Yuan, Q., Wang, S., & Peng, J. (2023). Operational efficiency optimisation method for ship fleet to comply with the carbon intensity indicator (CII) regulation. *Ocean Engineering, 286*, 115487. https://doi.org/10.1016/j.oceaneng.2023.115487

www.ingramcontent.com/pod-product-compliance
Lightning Source LLC
Chambersburg PA
CBHW080851120626
46546CB00008B/2784